I0814435

THE OFFICIAL BAKING BOOK

THE OFFICIAL BAKING BOOK

Recipes by Jenn Fujikawa

Written by Marc Sumerak

Based on *Avatar: The Last Airbender*

Created by Michael Dante DiMartino and Bryan Konietzko

SAN RAFAEL • LOS ANGELES • LONDON

CONTENTS

BOOK ONE

RECIPES FROM THE FIRST CHAPTER IN AVATAR AANG'S JOURNEY

BOOK TWO

RECIPES FROM THE SECOND CHAPTER IN AVATAR AANG'S JOURNEY

BOOK THREE

RECIPES FROM THE THIRD CHAPTER IN AVATAR AANG'S JOURNEY

INTRODUCTION

Balance. It's an important part of every aspect of life. It's especially important in cooking where too much or not enough of any ingredient can upset flavor and texture. Find your own form of balance in the kitchen with baking recipes inspired by Team Avatar's travels through the four nations.

Divided into three books, each section follows a season of stories in Avatar Aang's journey. Like him, you'll experiment with new techniques; experience moments salty, sweet, and savory; and pick up lessons from friends along the way. In Book One, you'll reunite with familiar figures: enjoying Jennamite Cookies in honor of Aang's old friend Bumi or Kyoshi Warriors Pastry Fans that would make Suki proud. In Book Two, you'll make new discoveries: like the frightening power of Azula's lightningbending, captured in a spice-forward scone. And in Book Three, you'll find yourself in the company of Old Masters with dishes like The Dancing Dragon Pineapple Buns and Lion Turtle Cream Puffs. Of course, in honor of Uncle Iroh, almost every one of the treats within these pages pairs perfectly with a nice cup of tea!

Baking is both a science and an art. It takes skill and discipline to get a recipe right, but you'll likely find your dishes come out best when you have fun with them—just like Team Avatar. Aang, Katara, Sokka, and Toph had to journey far and wide to develop the abilities they needed for the final battle against the Fire Lord, but that didn't mean there wasn't time for penguin sledding! In the same way, this book can be a guide as you hone your talents. But it's up to you to bring yourself to each bake. Whether you're learning the basics or on your way to becoming a master, remember that mistakes are part of the process. You might end up with sugar and flour in a colorful mess, but trying to achieve perfection right away would be like trying to learn airbending without rustling a few leaves.

So get ready to find balance—in your ingredients, in your kitchen, and in yourself. You're now on an exciting new journey toward a delicious destiny!

BOOK ONE

RECIPES FROM THE FIRST CHAPTER IN AVATAR AANG'S JOURNEY

Some have said that the Avatar disappeared when the world needed him most. Others believed the boy in the iceberg reemerged at the perfect time. Book One of Aang's story includes chance encounters and major moments when Team Avatar seems to be in the right place at the right time--including Aang's first visit to the Spirit World with Hei Bai and Sokka's first encounters with the Mechanist, who helped him discover his own inventive side.

Timing can make a huge difference in baking as well. A matter of minutes can make or break a recipe. But the act of showing up makes any moment the right one to start something new. Celebrate Team Avatar's unexpected discoveries and make a few of your own, with recipes that include Hei Bai Cookies and the Mechanist's Lunchtime Egg Pastry. Just as Team Avatar set out from the South Pole to learn all forms of bending, this is the perfect place and time to start (or pick up) your journey to become a baking master!

AANG CUPCAKES

V · PREP TIME: 30 minutes · COOK TIME: 17 minutes · YIELD: 12 cupcakes

After spending a century frozen inside of an iceberg, the Avatar was finally set free by two young members of the Water Tribe, Katara and Sokka. Almost immediately, Aang's optimism and love of life rubbed off on his new companions—and everyone who was part of his epic journey. These cupcakes capture Aang with his easy smile and make the perfect treat after a day of doing your Avatar thing, keeping the world safe.

CUPCAKES

1½ cups sifted cake flour

1 teaspoon baking powder

½ teaspoon ground cinnamon

¼ teaspoon ground nutmeg

¼ teaspoon kosher salt

½ cup (1 stick) unsalted butter

1 cup granulated sugar

2 large eggs

½ cup sour cream

1 teaspoon vanilla extract

¾ cup chocolate hazelnut spread

FROSTING

½ cup (1 stick) unsalted butter, softened

4 ounces cream cheese, softened

1½ cups powdered sugar

1 teaspoon vanilla extract

¼ teaspoon kosher salt

2 tablespoons heavy whipping cream

1 drop pink gel food coloring

DECORATION

Light blue fondant

Black fondant

SPECIAL EQUIPMENT

Cupcake pan

Cupcake liners

Stand mixer or handheld mixer

Wire rack

Piping bag and tips

Preheat the oven to 350°F. Prepare a cupcake pan with liners.

TO MAKE THE CUPCAKES:

In a medium bowl, whisk together the cake flour, baking powder, cinnamon, nutmeg, and salt. Set aside.

In the bowl of a stand mixer fitted with the paddle attachment (or in a large bowl with a handheld mixer) on medium speed, cream the butter and granulated sugar until fluffy. Add the eggs, sour cream, and vanilla. Slowly add the dry ingredients, until just combined. Spoon the batter into the liners.

Bake for 15 to 17 minutes, or until a toothpick inserted into the center of a cupcake comes out clean. Let cool on a wire rack.

Use a spoon to core out 1 tablespoon of cake from the center of each cupcake. Fill with the chocolate-hazelnut spread. Set aside.

TO MAKE THE FROSTING:

In a large bowl, using a handheld mixer on medium speed, cream the butter, cream cheese, powdered sugar, vanilla, and salt. Add the heavy whipping cream and pink gel food coloring and whip for 2 minutes, until light and fluffy.

Transfer ¼ cup of the frosting to a piping bag fitted with a small round tip. Set aside.

With the remaining frosting, frost the cupcakes. Use the frosting in the piping bag to pipe 1 small ear on each side of the head on all the frosted cupcakes.

TO MAKE THE DECORATIONS:

Roll out the light blue fondant to ⅛ inch thick. Cut out 12 arrow shapes and place one on the top half of each cupcake, pointing down.

Use small pieces of black fondant to create the eyebrows, eyes, and mouths. Add these to each cupcake, just under the arrows.

APPA FOOTPRINT BUNS

PREP TIME: 3 hours · COOK TIME: 25 minutes · YIELD: 8 buns

Aang's companion for life, Appa, is a sky bison with a heart almost as big as his body. When not soaring through the skies as his friends' primary mode of transportation, this "ten-ton magical monster" (as Sokka called him) roams the Earth on his six powerful legs. These Chinese-style hot dog buns, in the shape of the giant footprints Appa left in his wake, pay homage to a cuddly creature who leaves quite an impression.

BUNS

1 envelope (2¼ teaspoons) active dry yeast

¾ cup whole milk, heated to 110°F

¼ cup sugar

½ teaspoon kosher salt

½ cup heavy cream, at room temperature

1 large egg

3 cups bread flour, plus more for dusting

2 tablespoons olive oil, for greasing

4 hot dogs

EGG WASH

1 large egg

1 tablespoon water

1 green onion, minced

1 teaspoon sesame seeds

SIMPLE SYRUP

2 tablespoons sugar

2 tablespoons boiling water

SPECIAL EQUIPMENT

Stand mixer

Pastry brush

Wire rack

TO MAKE THE BUNS:

In the bowl of a stand mixer fitted with a dough hook, sprinkle the yeast over the warm milk and let sit for 5 minutes, until foamy.

Add the sugar, salt, heavy cream, and egg and mix until combined. Slowly add the flour and mix until combined. Knead for 8 to 10 minutes until smooth and elastic.

Place the dough into a large bowl greased with oil, turning to coat. Cover with plastic wrap and let rise for 1½ hours, until doubled in size.

Punch down the dough, then turn out onto a lightly floured surface. Divide the dough in half, reserving one half.

With the other half, divide into 4 equal portions. Take one piece and roll it out the length of a hot dog. Place a hot dog in the center and wrap the dough around it, pinching the seams closed. Repeat with the remaining 3 hot dogs. Cut each wrapped hot dog into 6 equal pieces.

Divide the reserved dough half into 8 equal dough balls.

On 2 parchment-lined baking sheets, place the dough balls, 4 per sheet. Arrange 3 of the wrapped hot dog pieces, cut sides up, along the top of one ball to form a paw shape. Repeat with the remaining dough balls and cut hot dogs. Cover the baking sheets with towels and let rise for another hour.

Preheat the oven to 350°F.

TO MAKE THE EGG WASH:

In a small bowl, whisk together the egg and water. Brush the egg wash onto the buns. Sprinkle with the green onions and sesame seeds.

Bake for 22 to 25 minutes, until golden brown.

TO MAKE THE SIMPLE SYRUP:

In a small bowl, stir together the sugar and water. Immediately brush this onto the hot buns. Let cool on a wire rack.

MOMO MERINGUES

GF, V · PREP TIME: 2 hours · COOK TIME: 1 hour, plus 1½ hours to dry · YIELD: 12 cookies

From the day Team Avatar discovered this little lemur at the Southern Air Temple, Momo made a huge impact on his new friends. Sure, Sokka wanted to eat him at first, but it's a good thing he didn't, as Momo would go on to play a critical role in so many of their adventures. Plus, who wants to eat a lemur when you could have these adorable meringues instead?!

4 egg whites, at room temperature

½ teaspoon cream of tartar

1 cup powdered sugar

½ teaspoon clear vanilla extract

2 teaspoons unsweetened cocoa powder

12 pink heart sprinkles

BLACK ROYAL ICING

1 cup powdered sugar

1 teaspoon meringue powder

1 to 2 tablespoons warm water

4 drops black food gel coloring

¼ teaspoon clear vanilla extract

SPECIAL EQUIPMENT

Piping bags and tips

Wire rack

Preheat the oven to 200°F. Line 2 baking sheets with parchment.

In a large bowl, with a handheld mixer on high speed, whip the egg whites and cream of tartar for 3 to 5 minutes, until foamy.

Sprinkle in the powdered sugar 1 tablespoon at a time while continuing to whip until stiff peaks form. Add the clear vanilla and mix until combined.

Divide the meringue mixture in half, between 2 medium bowls. Leave one bowl as is. To the other medium bowl of meringue mixture, gently fold in the cocoa powder until the mixture is light brown. Transfer the meringue mixtures to separate piping bags.

On one of the prepared baking sheets, pipe the white meringue into twelve 2½-inch circles for Momo's head. Then pipe out 2-inch-long cone shapes on both sides to create Momo's ears.

Use the brown meringue to create the face and fill in the ears. Add a pink heart sprinkle for the mouth. Repeat with the remaining meringue and sprinkles to create 11 more meringue cookies.

Bake for 1 hour, until the meringue cookies are dry. Turn the oven off, keep the oven door closed, and leave in the oven for another 1½ hours to dry completely.

Remove the cookies from the baking sheets and let cool completely on a wire rack.

TO MAKE THE BLACK ROYAL ICING:
In a medium bowl with a handheld mixer on medium speed, mix together the powdered sugar and meringue powder. Add half the water, the black gel food coloring, and the clear vanilla and whisk until combined. Gradually add the remaining water as needed, and whisk for 2 minutes, until thickened. Transfer to a piping bag.

Use the black icing to create Momo's eyes and nose. Let the icing dry before serving.

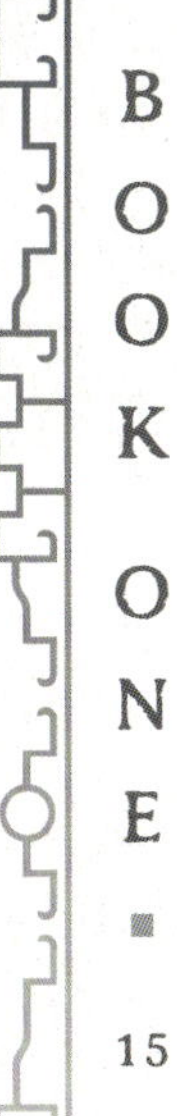

TRAVEL-SIZE AIR NOMAD FRUIT PIES

V · PREP TIME: 1 hour, plus 2 hours chilling time · COOK TIME: 30 minutes · YIELD: 12 mini pies

Even before Aang was identified as the Avatar, his fellow Air Nomads were already known for many amazing things—including their ancient cake-making techniques. According to Aang's mentor, Monk Gyatso, the secret of these fruit pies is in their gooey centers. This recipe takes the original concept and makes them miniature: the perfect size for sharing with your own team of heroes, especially when you're off on an adventure and need to pack light. (Just try not to hurl them onto anyone's head during training sessions!)

CRUST

1 cup finely ground graham cracker crumbs

2 tablespoons light brown sugar

½ teaspoon ground cinnamon

4 tablespoons unsalted butter, melted

BATTER

16 ounces cream cheese

1 cup granulated sugar

1 tablespoon lemon zest

1 teaspoon vanilla extract

¼ teaspoon kosher salt

2 large eggs

Preheat the oven to 325°F. Coat a muffin pan with nonstick spray.

TO MAKE THE CRUST:

In a small bowl, stir the graham cracker crumbs, brown sugar, cinnamon, and butter until combined. Divide the mixture evenly among the cups of the prepared muffin pan, and press firmly into the bottom of each cup.

TO MAKE THE BATTER:

In the bowl of a stand mixer fitted with the paddle attachment (or in a large bowl with a handheld mixer) on medium speed, cream the cream cheese, granulated sugar, lemon zest, vanilla, and salt. Add the eggs one at a time, and beat until smooth. Spoon the batter evenly over the crusts.

Bake for 18 to 20 minutes, until just set. Let cool completely. Refrigerate for 2 hours, until chilled.

FROSTING

1 cup granulated sugar

⅓ cup water

¼ teaspoon cream of tartar

2 large egg whites

1 teaspoon vanilla extract

2 drops orange gel food coloring

2 drops red gel food coloring

1 teaspoon ube extract

2 drops yellow gel food coloring

TOPPINGS

2 tablespoons apricot preserves

2 tablespoons strawberry jam

2 tablespoons blackberry jam

2 tablespoons lemon curd

SPECIAL EQUIPMENT

Muffin pan

Stand mixer or handheld mixer

Piping bags and tips

Candy thermometer

TO MAKE THE FROSTING:

In a medium saucepan over medium heat, heat the granulated sugar, water, and cream of tartar for 2 to 3 minutes, until the sugar has dissolved and the hot syrup starts to bubble, and a candy thermometer reaches 238°F to 245°F. Turn off the heat.

In the bowl of a stand mixer fitted with the whisk attachment (or in a large bowl with a handheld mixer) on medium-high speed, whip the egg whites until foamy. Slowly add the hot syrup, continuing to whip until stiff peaks form, about 10 minutes, until thickened. Add the vanilla and mix until combined.

Divide the frosting among 4 separate bowls. Stir the orange gel food coloring into one bowl to tint the frosting a pastel orange shade. Add the red gel food coloring to the second bowl, tinting it a dark pink color. Add the ube extract to the third bowl, to create a pastel purple color. Finally, stir the yellow gel food coloring into the last bowl, to create a pastel yellow shade. Place each frosting into a piping bag. Set aside.

TO MAKE THE TOPPING:

Spoon a dollop of the apricot preserves onto the tops of 3 cheesecakes. Then pipe the orange frosting over the preserves, covering completely.

With the next 3 cheesecakes, repeat the process using the strawberry jam. Spoon it onto the tops of the cheesecakes, then pipe the dark pink frosting to cover the jam. Repeat the process with the blackberry jam and ube frosting. Then do the same with the lemon curd and the yellow frosting. Refrigerate until ready to serve.

DESSERT FOR BREAKFAST

V · PREP TIME: 15 minutes · COOK TIME: 1 hour · YIELD: 10 servings

When the citizens of Kyoshi Island realized that Aang was the Avatar, they welcomed him and his friends with a massive spread of food, including all sorts of sugary confections. Aang was thrilled to be having "dessert for breakfast" . . . which isn't everyone's cup of tea. You can make the call for yourself with this recipe, which combines flour and ice cream to create your own ice cream bread. It's a sweet treat to enjoy whenever *you* choose.

BREAD LOAF

1 pint strawberry ice cream, melted

3 cups self-rising flour, divided

1 pint chocolate ice cream, melted

GLAZE

¾ cup powdered sugar

¼ cup unsweetened cocoa powder

1 tablespoon unsalted butter, melted

½ teaspoon vanilla extract

1½ tablespoons whole milk

2 tablespoons crushed freeze-dried strawberries

SPECIAL EQUIPMENT

Instant-read thermometer

9-by-5-inch loaf pan

Preheat the oven to 350°F.

Grease a 9-by-5-inch loaf pan with nonstick spray.

TO MAKE THE BREAD LOAF:

In a medium bowl, stir the melted strawberry ice cream and 1½ cups of the flour until just combined. In a second medium bowl, stir the melted chocolate ice cream and the remaining 1½ cups of flour until just combined. Scoop the batters, alternating between them, into the prepped loaf pan.

Bake for 45 to 50 minutes, or until it reaches an internal temperature of 190°F on an instant-read thermometer. Remove from the oven and let cool completely. Remove the cake from the pan and place on a serving platter.

TO MAKE THE GLAZE:

In a small bowl, whisk together the powdered sugar, cocoa powder, melted butter, and vanilla. Stir in the milk until combined. Drizzle the glaze over the cake. Sprinkle with the freeze-dried strawberries.

SOKKA'S SAVORY BOOMERANGS

PREP TIME: 30 minutes · COOK TIME: 12 minutes · YIELD: 48 wontons

Sokka of the Southern Water Tribe may not have been able to bend water like his sister, Katara, but that doesn't mean he is without resources to draw on. Sokka's tool of choice, his trusty boomerang, is a signature of sorts, like the arrow tattoo on Aang's forehead or Katara's "hair loopies." These baked veggie wontons will make you feel like a boomerang yourself: you'll keep coming back for more!

WONTONS

1 tablespoon olive oil

2 cloves garlic, minced

1 teaspoon minced fresh ginger

1 pound ground pork

4 ounces mushrooms, minced

2 green onions, diced

3 tablespoons oyster sauce

2 tablespoons soy sauce

1 teaspoon rice vinegar

1 teaspoon sesame oil

½ teaspoon ground white pepper

4 ounces cooked shrimp, diced

48 square wonton wrappers

EGG WASH

1 egg

1 tablespoon water

SPECIAL EQUIPMENT

Pastry brush

Fine-mesh strainer

Wire rack

TO MAKE THE WONTONS:

In a large skillet over medium-high heat, heat the olive oil. Add the garlic and ginger. Cook, stirring, for about 30 seconds, until fragrant.

Add the pork, mushrooms, green onions, oyster sauce, soy sauce, rice vinegar, sesame oil, and white pepper. Cook for 4 to 6 minutes, until the pork is no longer pink. Stir in the diced shrimp and cook for 1 to 2 minutes more, until warmed through. Transfer to a fine-mesh strainer set over a bowl to drain the excess liquid. Let cool.

TO MAKE THE EGG WASH:

In a small bowl, whisk together the egg and water.

Place 1 tablespoon of filling in the center of a wonton wrapper. Brush the egg wash onto the edges of the wrapper. Bring two of the corners together to form a point, and then pinch to seal down the edges, forming a triangle. Place on a parchment-lined plate and cover with a towel. Repeat with the rest of the filling and wrappers.

Preheat the oven to 400°F. Place a wire rack on top of a baking sheet and coat it with nonstick spray.

Place the wontons onto the prepared rack. Spray the wontons with nonstick spray. Bake for 12 to 14 minutes, until golden brown.

KYOSHI WARRIORS PASTRY FANS

V · PREP TIME: 2 hours 30 minutes · COOK TIME: 25 minutes · YIELD: 8 pastries

While Aang received a warm welcome from Kyoshi Island's locals, Sokka got to know their elite squad of soldiers, the Kyoshi Warriors. Brave and honorable fighters, the women of the island train for years in a distinct form of combat, using beautiful fans as powerful weapons that can turn an opponent's force back against them. These filled pastries are folded to resemble the signature weapon of the Kyoshi Warriors. Like the warriors themselves, they are not to be underestimated.

PASTRY

1 envelope (2¼ teaspoons) active dry yeast

1 cup whole milk, heated to 110°F

¼ cup shortening

2 tablespoons sugar

2 tablespoons honey

½ teaspoon kosher salt

1 large egg

3 cups all-purpose flour, plus more for dusting

2 tablespoons olive oil, for greasing

1½ cups red bean paste, divided into 8 balls

EGG WASH

1 large egg

1 tablespoon water

SIMPLE SYRUP

2 tablespoons sugar

2 tablespoons boiling water

SPECIAL EQUIPMENT

Stand mixer

Pastry brush

Wire rack

TO MAKE THE PASTRY:

In the bowl of a stand mixer fitted with a dough hook, sprinkle the yeast over the warm milk and let sit for 10 minutes, until foamy.

With the mixer on medium speed, add the shortening, sugar, honey, salt, and egg and mix until combined. Turn the mixer speed to low and slowly add the flour until combined. Increase the mixer to medium-high speed and knead the dough for 5 to 8 minutes, until it is smooth and elastic.

Place the dough in a large bowl greased with olive oil, turning to coat. Cover with plastic wrap and let rise for 1½ hours, until doubled in size.

Preheat the oven to 350°F. Line a baking sheet with parchment paper.

Punch down the dough, then turn out onto a lightly floured surface. Divide the dough into 8 equal balls.

Roll out one ball of dough into a 5-inch circle. Place a ball of red bean paste into the center. Pull up the dough around the filling and pinch the edges to seal. Flatten the ball out into a 4-inch circle. With a sharp knife, make 4 equally spaced cuts from the edge inward, keeping the center intact. Add 4 more cuts in between, creating 8 pieces in total. Twist the outer edges of each piece clockwise and upward to show off the red bean. Pull the bottom pieces straight across, to create a fan shape. Transfer to the prepped baking sheet. Repeat with the remaining dough balls and red bean paste.

TO MAKE THE EGG WASH:

In a small bowl, whisk together the egg and water. Brush the egg wash onto the buns.

Bake for 20 minutes, until golden brown.

TO MAKE THE SIMPLE SYRUP:

In a small bowl, stir together the sugar and water. Immediately brush onto the hot buns. Let cool on a wire rack.

ELEPHANT-KOI COOKIES

V · PREP TIME: 40 minutes · COOK TIME: 10 minutes · YIELD: 24 cookies

The waters surrounding Kyoshi Island are home to a number of unique sea-dwelling species, including the enormous elephant-koi. Aang loves to grab onto the fins of these fancy fish and surf on their backs. Of course, what started as fun eventually drew the attention of a very hungry sea monster called the unagi. These cookies aren't as big as an actual elephant-koi, but they're still likely to satisfy everyone, even if they have unagi-size appetites!

3 cups all-purpose flour, plus more for dusting
½ teaspoon baking powder
¼ teaspoon kosher salt
1 cup (2 sticks) unsalted butter, softened
1 cup sugar
1 large egg
1 teaspoon vanilla extract
Orange gel food coloring
Yellow gel food coloring
Edible silver color mist

BLACK ROYAL ICING

1 cup powdered sugar
1 teaspoon meringue powder
1 to 2 tablespoons warm water
4 drops black food gel coloring
¼ teaspoon clear vanilla extract

SPECIAL EQUIPMENT

Stand mixer or handheld mixer
Wire rack

In a medium bowl, whisk together the flour, baking powder, and salt. Set aside.

In the bowl of a stand mixer fitted with the paddle attachment (or in a large bowl with a handheld mixer) on medium speed, cream the butter and sugar until fluffy. Add the egg and vanilla, mixing until just combined. Add the flour mixture and beat until just combined. Divide the dough in half, leaving one half in the bowl, and remove and set aside the other half.

To the dough in the bowl, add the orange gel food coloring and mix on low speed until bright orange. Remove and wrap in plastic wrap.

Wash and dry the mixing bowl and paddle attachment. Replace onto the mixer and add the reserved dough half to the bowl. Add the yellow gel food coloring and mix on low speed until bright yellow. Wrap in plastic wrap. Refrigerate both doughs for 20 minutes.

Preheat the oven to 350°F. Line 2 baking sheets with parchment paper.

On a lightly floured surface, drop pieces of orange and yellow dough to form a pattern. Roll out to make a single dough ¼ inch thick.

Cut out koi shapes using the below template.Use the edge of a piping tip to make "scales" along each koi's back. Transfer to the prepared baking sheets. Reroll the scraps and repeat until all the dough has been used.

Bake for 10 minutes, until lightly browned and the edges are firm. Let cool on a wire rack. Lightly spray the cookies with edible silver mist.

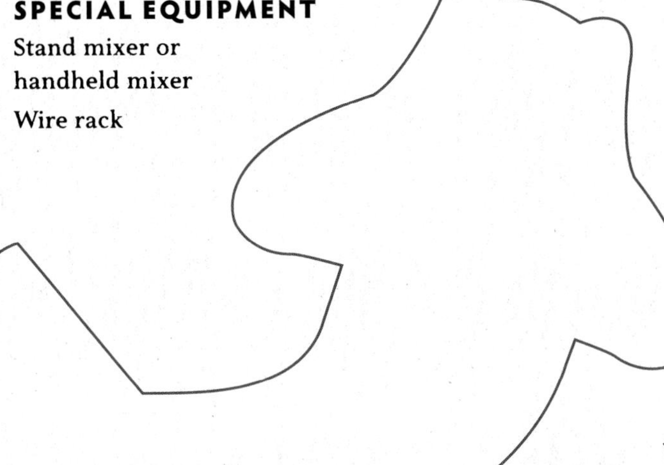

TO MAKE THE BLACK ROYAL ICING: In a medium bowl with a handheld mixer on low speed, mix together the powdered sugar and meringue powder. Add half the water, the black gel food coloring, and the clear vanilla and mix until combined. Raise the speed to medium. Gradually add the remaining water as needed, and mix for 2 minutes, until thickened. Transfer to a piping bag.

Use black icing to create an eye on each side of the head and the mouth whiskers. Let the icing dry.

MY CABBAGE BITES!

V · PREP TIME: 30 minutes · COOK TIME: 15 minutes · YIELD: 20 cake bites

Team Avatar encountered many colorful characters during their travels, but none were quite so unhappy to see them as one unfortunate cabbage merchant. Each time he crossed paths with Aang and his crew, his cart full of cabbages became a casualty in the chaos. These chocolate cake bites are a delicious tribute to the many leafy green heads our beloved merchant lost along the way.

CAKES

1 cup all-purpose flour

¼ cup packed light brown sugar

¼ cup granulated sugar

¼ cup unsweetened cocoa powder

1 teaspoon baking powder

¼ teaspoon kosher salt

4 tablespoons unsalted butter, softened

1 large egg

⅔ cup whole milk

½ teaspoon vanilla extract

⅓ cup mini chocolate chips

DECORATIONS

10 ounces green fondant

Cornstarch, for dusting

FROSTING

½ cup (1 stick) unsalted butter, softened

1½ cups powdered sugar

1 tablespoon cocoa powder

2 teaspoons whole milk

¼ cup chocolate cookie crumbs

SPECIAL EQUIPMENT

Muffin pan

Stand mixer or handheld mixer

Piping bags and tips

Wire rack

Preheat the oven to 325°F. Grease a mini muffin pan with nonstick spray.

TO MAKE THE CAKES:

In a large bowl, whisk together the flour, brown sugar, granulated sugar, cocoa powder, baking powder, and salt. Make a well in the center of the dry ingredients, add the butter, egg, milk, and vanilla, and whisk until combined. Fold in the mini chocolate chips. Transfer the batter to a piping bag and pipe into the prepared pan.

Bake for 15 to 17 minutes, until a toothpick inserted into the center of the cake bites comes out clean. Let cool on a wire rack.

TO MAKE THE DECORATIONS:

Take 1 teaspoon of fondant and roll it into a small ball. On a clean surface dusted with cornstarch, roll out the fondant ball to 1/8 inch thick and form into a small curved leaf shape. Repeat to create 10 leaves. Take one leaf and wrap a second leaf around the base. Repeat around the leaves in a circle. Pinch the bottom, then fan out the leaves to form a cabbage shape. Repeat with the fondant to create 20 small fondant cabbages.

TO MAKE THE FROSTING:

In the bowl of a stand mixer fitted with the paddle attachment (or in a large bowl with a handheld mixer) on medium speed, cream the butter, powdered sugar, and cocoa powder until fluffy. Add the milk and beat until combined. Transfer to a piping bag fitted with a star tip.

Pipe the frosting onto the cake bites. Sprinkle with the cookie crumbs. Add a fondant cabbage to each cake bite.

JENNAMITE COOKIES

V · PREP TIME: 40 minutes · COOK TIME: 10 minutes · YIELD: 30 cookies

In Omashu, King Bumi tasked Aang with a series of challenges and an extremely stressful time frame: he had to pass these tests while his friends were encased in a strange, creeping crystal called Jennamite. Later, Bumi revealed that Jennamite was really a kind of rock candy, making Sokka and Katara's fate sound more delicious than deadly. A batch of these cookies, topped with crunchy shards of rock candy, will have everyone thinking you're a mad genius!

COOKIES

3 cups all-purpose flour
½ teaspoon baking powder
¼ teaspoon kosher salt
1 cup (2 sticks) unsalted butter, softened
½ cup packed light brown sugar
½ cup granulated sugar
1 large egg
1 teaspoon almond extract

ICING

1 cup powdered sugar
2 tablespoons whole milk
1 tablespoon unsalted butter, melted
1 teaspoon vanilla extract
2 drops green gel food coloring
2 drops purple gel food coloring

TOPPING

½ cup green sugar crystals
¼ cup green popping candy
½ cup purple sugar crystals
¼ cup purple popping candy

SPECIAL EQUIPMENT

Stand mixer or handheld mixer
Wire rack

TO MAKE THE COOKIES:

In a medium bowl, whisk together the flour, baking powder, and salt. Set aside.

In the bowl of a stand mixer fitted with the paddle attachment (or in a large bowl with a handheld mixer) on medium speed, cream the butter, brown sugar, and granulated sugar until combined. Add the egg and almond extract and beat until just combined. Add the flour mixture and mix until just combined. Divide the dough in half.

Lay out 2 large sheets of plastic wrap. Transfer each dough half to a sheet, wrap them tightly, and refrigerate for 20 minutes.

Preheat the oven to 350°F. Line 2 or 3 baking sheets with parchment paper.

Roll out the dough to ⅜ inch thick. Cut out approximately 30 random rectangular shapes and place on the prepared baking sheets.

Bake for 10 minutes, until lightly browned and the edges are firm. Let cool on a wire rack.

TO MAKE THE ICING:

In a medium bowl, stir together the powdered sugar, milk, butter, and vanilla until combined. Divide into 2 bowls. Use the green gel food coloring to dye the first bowl of icing. Use the purple gel food coloring to dye the second bowl.

TO MAKE THE TOPPING:

For 15 of the cookies, dip the top of the cookies into the green icing. Then coat in green sugar crystals. Sprinkle on the green popping candy. Let dry on a wire rack.

Repeat the same process with the remaining 15 cookies, using the purple icing, purple sugar crystals, and purple popping candy. Let dry on a wire rack.

UPSIDE-DOWN MOON PEACH CAKES

V · PREP TIME: 15 minutes · COOK TIME: 20 minutes · YIELD: 12 cakes

Momo and Appa may eat pretty much anything they can get their paws on, but there are few things they love as much as moon peaches. These individual peach upside-down cakes are perfect for any occasion, whether you're celebrating the winter solstice or just lounging around with your best buddies.

TOPPING

6 tablespoons unsalted butter, melted

⅓ cup packed light brown sugar

2 peaches, pitted, peeled, and cut into 24 slices

CAKES

2 cups all-purpose flour

1 teaspoon baking powder

1 teaspoon ground cinnamon

¼ teaspoon ground nutmeg

¼ teaspoon kosher salt

1 cup (2 sticks) unsalted butter, softened

½ cup granulated sugar

¼ cup packed light brown sugar

2 large eggs

1 tablespoon lemon juice

1 teaspoon vanilla extract

⅔ cup buttermilk

SPECIAL EQUIPMENT

Muffin pan

Stand mixer or handheld mixer

Preheat the oven to 350°F.

TO MAKE THE TOPPING:

Pour the melted butter into the cups of the muffin pan, brushing it up the sides. Add the brown sugar. Place 2 peach slices into each cup on top of the sugar.

TO MAKE THE CAKES:

In a large bowl, whisk together the flour, baking powder, cinnamon, nutmeg, and salt.

In the bowl of a stand mixer fitted with the paddle attachment (or in a large bowl with a handheld mixer) on medium speed, cream the butter, granulated sugar, and brown sugar for 5 minutes, until fluffy. Add the eggs, lemon juice, and vanilla and beat until just combined. Alternate adding the dry mixture with the buttermilk, adding both in phases and beating until smooth. Spoon batter into the prepared tin, covering the arranged peach halves.

Bake for 20 minutes, until a toothpick inserted into each cake comes out clean. Let cool in the pan for 20 minutes. Run a knife around the edge of the pan to loosen the cakes, then turn out onto a plate.

BISON WHISTLE BISCOTTI

V · PREP TIME: 1 hour 40 minutes · COOK TIME: 1 hour · YIELD: 18 biscotti

For a trinket that cost one copper piece at a merchants' pier, Aang's bison whistle has come in handy on many occasions. Not only can it summon Appa, but it can also call all of the animals in the Ba Sing Se Zoo at the same time. Not bad for something Sokka thought was just a piece of junk! These cookies capture the bison whistle's classic shape—and sound just the same to a human!

CHOCOLATE HORNS

2 ounces dark chocolate

½ teaspoon coconut oil

BISCOTTI

¾ cup slivered almonds

2¼ cups all-purpose flour

1 teaspoon baking powder

½ teaspoon ground cinnamon

¼ teaspoon kosher salt

½ cup (1 stick) unsalted butter, softened

1 cup sugar

2 large eggs, at room temperature

1 teaspoon almond extract

½ teaspoon vanilla extract

COATING

8 ounces white chocolate

½ cup shredded coconut

SPECIAL EQUIPMENT

Stand mixer

Wire rack

Double boiler

TO MAKE THE CHOCOLATE HORNS:

Line a small baking sheet with parchment paper.

In a microwave-safe bowl, microwave the dark chocolate for 30 seconds. Stir and microwave in 15-second increments until melted. Stir in the coconut oil until combined. Use a small spoon to create 1-inch horn shapes on the parchment paper. Freeze until ready to use.

TO MAKE THE BISCOTTI:

Preheat the oven to 325°F. Line 2 baking sheets with parchment paper. Spread the almonds evenly on one of the prepared baking sheets. Bake for 10 minutes, until lightly golden. Let cool.

In a large bowl, whisk together the flour, baking powder, cinnamon, and salt. Set aside.

In the bowl of a stand mixer fitted with the paddle attachment (or in a large bowl with a handheld mixer) on medium speed, cream the butter and sugar until fluffy. Add the eggs, almond extract, and vanilla and beat until just combined. Add the dry ingredients and beat until combined. Fold in the toasted almonds.

On the remaining prepared baking sheet, divide the dough in half and shape into 2 logs about 1 inch thick. Refrigerate for 15 minutes.

Preheat the oven to 325°F.

Bake for 25 minutes, until just set. Let cool for 10 minutes.

Transfer to a cutting board and slice each log into nine ½-inch-wide slices. Place the slices back on the prepared baking sheets.

Bake for another 25 minutes, until golden brown. Let cool on a wire rack.

TO MAKE THE COATING:

To the base of a double boiler, add 2 inches of water. Bring to a low simmer over medium heat. Place the top part of the double boiler over the water. Add the white chocolate. Stir until melted.

Spoon the melted chocolate over the curved part of the biscotti. Top with the coconut and place on the parchment. Add the dark chocolate horns. Let the chocolate set.

TSUNGI HORNS

V · PREP TIME: 30 minutes · COOK TIME: 20 minutes · YIELD: 9 horns

While accompanying his nephew Prince Zuko on a quest to find the Avatar, former Fire Nation General Iroh bought a tsungi horn to play on their ship's music night. Sadly, these cream-filled pastry horns won't make beautiful music if you try to play them (just trust us on that one), but they are nice to munch on while your own crew sings stirring love songs. On that note, we hear secret tunnels make for a perfectly lyrical setting . . .

PASTRY HORNS

One 8.5-ounce sheet puff pastry, thawed

1 large egg

1 tablespoon water

¼ cup coarse sanding sugar

CREAM FILLING

4 ounces mascarpone cheese

½ cup powdered sugar, plus more for dusting

1 tablespoon lemon zest

½ teaspoon vanilla extract

¾ cup heavy whipping cream

SPECIAL EQUIPMENT

Nine 5-inch-long metal pastry cone molds

Stand mixer or handheld mixer

Pastry brush

Piping bag and star tip

TO MAKE THE PASTRY HORNS:

Grease nine 5-inch-long metal pastry cones with nonstick spray. Set aside.

Cut the puff pastry into 1-inch-wide strips. Wind each strip around a cone, overlapping the pastry strips as you go. Pinch the tip at the end to close. Repeat with the other 8 cones. Cover with plastic wrap and refrigerate for 20 minutes.

Preheat the oven to 400°F. Line a baking sheet with parchment paper.

In a small bowl, whisk together the egg and water. Use a pastry brush to brush the horns with the egg wash. Sprinkle with the sanding sugar. Place on the prepared baking sheet.

Bake for 15 to 18 minutes, until golden brown. Let cool on the metal forms.

TO MAKE THE CREAM FILLING:

In a medium bowl, stir together the mascarpone cheese, ½ cup powdered sugar, lemon zest, and vanilla until smooth. Set aside.

In a stand mixer fitted with the whisk attachment (or in a large bowl with a handheld mixer) on medium-high speed, whip the whipping cream until stiff peaks form. Fold in the mascarpone mixture until combined. Transfer to a piping bag fitted with a large star tip.

Remove the pastry horns from the metal cones and pipe the cream filling into each pastry, distributing it evenly among the horns. Dust with more powdered sugar just before serving.

BLASTING JELLY CAKES

PREP TIME: 40 minutes · COOK TIME: 20 minutes · YIELD: 24 servings

When Jet and his Freedom Fighters raided a Fire Nation camp, they recovered barrels of blasting jelly and boxes of jellied candy. Both of those were good scores . . . but ones that you probably wouldn't want to get mixed up. These lamingtons bring together the best of both worlds, bursting with jelly in every bite. It's an explosion of flavor that won't leave you questioning whether you've chosen the right path.

CAKE

2 cups cake flour

1½ teaspoons baking powder

¼ teaspoon kosher salt

1 cup (2 sticks) unsalted butter, softened

1 cup sugar

3 large eggs, separated

1 teaspoon vanilla extract

½ cup whole milk

COATING

3 ounces strawberry gelatin

½ cup boiling water

½ cup strawberry jam

¼ cup cold water

2 cups desiccated coconut

SPECIAL EQUIPMENT

13-by-9-inch pan

Stand mixer or handheld mixer

Fine-mesh strainer

Wire rack

Preheat the oven to 350°F. Line a 13 by 9 inch pan with parchment paper and then coat with nonstick spray.

TO MAKE THE CAKE:

In a large bowl, whisk together the cake flour, baking powder, and salt. Set aside.

In the bowl of a stand mixer fitted with the paddle attachment (or in a large bowl with a handheld mixer) on medium speed, cream the butter, sugar, egg yolks, and vanilla until light in color. Add the dry mixture and the milk, alternating between the two, and beat until just combined. Set aside.

In a separate bowl, whip the egg whites until stiff peaks form. Fold into the batter until combined. Pour the batter into the prepared pan.

Bake for 20 minutes, until a toothpick inserted into the center of the cake comes out clean. Let cool completely.

TO MAKE THE COATING:

In a medium bowl, stir together the strawberry gelatin and boiling water until the gelatin has dissolved. Stir in the strawberry jam and cold water until combined. Pour through a fine-mesh strainer set over a separate bowl. Set aside.

Place the coconut into a medium bowl.

Turn out the cake onto a cutting board and remove the parchment paper. Trim the edges of the cooled cake and cut it into 24 equal pieces.

Dip the cake into the strawberry mixture, then roll in the coconut. Place on a wire rack for 15 minutes to set.

LYCHEE PAVLOVA

GF, V · PREP TIME: 30 minutes, plus 2 hours resting · COOK TIME: 1 hour and 45 minutes · YIELD: 8 servings

During a long, hungry journey across a nearly endless canyon, Aang mused that he could eat his weight in lychee nuts. Who could blame him? They're so delectable that the Fire Nation uses them as bait in their hunting traps throughout forests (as Momo discovered the hard way). This oven-baked pavlova, topped with fruit and lychee, is a dessert no one will be able to resist. Approach this one with caution . . . just in case . . .

PAVLOVA

4 large egg whites

½ teaspoon cream of tartar

1 cup granulated sugar

1 teaspoon cornstarch

½ teaspoon white vinegar

WHIPPED CREAM

1½ cups heavy whipping cream

⅔ cup powdered sugar

½ teaspoon clear vanilla extract

¼ teaspoon kosher salt

TOPPING

One 20-ounce can lychees, drained

6 ounces raspberries

3 ounces blueberries

1 tablespoon lime zest

SPECIAL EQUIPMENT

Stand mixer or handheld mixer

Preheat the oven to 250°F. Line a baking sheet with parchment paper.

TO MAKE THE PAVLOVA:
In a stand mixer fitted with the whisk attachment (or in a large bowl with a handheld mixer) on medium-high speed, whip the egg whites and cream of tartar for 2 to 3 minutes, until stiff peaks form. Slowly sprinkle in the granulated sugar and whip until just combined. Turn the speed up to high and whip for 4 to 5 minutes, until glossy peaks form. Fold in the cornstarch and white vinegar.

Spoon the meringue into an 8-inch circle on the prepared baking sheet. Bake for 1 hour and 45 minutes, until lightly browned. Turn the oven off and keep the door closed. Let sit for 2 hours.

Remove the pavlova from the baking sheet and transfer to a serving dish.

TO MAKE THE WHIPPED CREAM:
In a stand mixer fitted with the whisk attachment (or in a large bowl with a handheld mixer) on medium-high speed, whip the heavy cream for 2 minutes, until soft peaks form. Slowly add the powdered sugar, clear vanilla, and salt. Whip for 1 minute more, until thickened. Spoon the whipped cream onto the pavlova.

TO MAKE THE TOPPING:
Arrange the lychees, raspberries, and blueberries on top of the cream. Sprinkle with the lime zest. Serve immediately.

FLAMING FIRE FLAKES COOKIES

V · PREP TIME: 15 minutes · COOK TIME: 10 minutes · YIELD: 24 cookies

The Fire Days Festival is a celebration of the Fire Nation, with cultural exhibits, performers, and vendors selling all sorts of traditional delicacies—including a favorite Fire Nation snack, Flaming Fire Flakes! These cayenne and cornflake cookies capture the heat and crunch of Flaming Fire Flakes in a whole new form. You don't have to be a firebender to enjoy these blazing biscuits—but if you're not, you might want to have a cool drink handy . . .

- 2 cups all-purpose flour
- 1 teaspoon baking soda
- 1 teaspoon ground cinnamon
- ½ teaspoon cayenne pepper
- ½ teaspoon ground nutmeg
- ¼ teaspoon ground cloves
- 1 cup (2 sticks) unsalted butter, softened
- ½ cup granulated sugar
- ¼ cup packed light brown sugar
- 1 teaspoon vanilla extract
- 1 large egg
- 1 cup crushed cornflakes
- 1 cup crushed hot puff snacks

SPECIAL EQUIPMENT

Stand mixer or handheld mixer

Wire rack

Preheat the oven to 350°F. Line 2 baking sheets with parchment paper.

In a large bowl, whisk together the flour, baking soda, cinnamon, cayenne, nutmeg, and cloves. Set aside.

In the bowl of a stand mixer fitted with the paddle attachment (or in a large bowl with a handheld mixer) on medium speed, cream the butter, granulated sugar, and brown sugar until fluffy. Add the vanilla and egg and beat until combined. Add the dry ingredient mix to the butter mixture, beating until just combined. Fold in the cornflakes.

Place the crushed puff snacks in a bowl. Roll the cookies into 24 balls, then roll in the crushed hot puff snacks. Place on the prepared baking sheets.

Bake for 12 minutes, until lightly browned. Let cool on a wire rack.

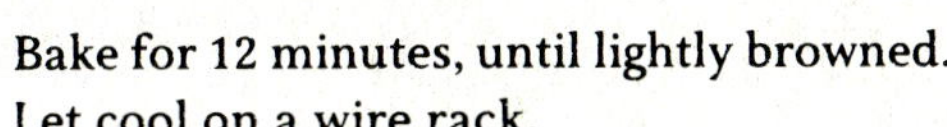

GAN JIN BREAD

V · PREP TIME: 3 hours · COOK TIME: 25 minutes · YIELD: 12 rolls

Those planning to cross the Great Divide, the largest canyon in the Earth Kingdom, should always listen to their guide and leave any food behind so that they don't attract dangerous predators. Of course, for rolls as delicious as these—inspired by the bread that the Gan Jin clan smuggled along with them—it might actually be worth facing off against some canyon crawlers!

ROLLS

1 envelope (2¼ teaspoons) active dry yeast

¾ cup whole milk, heated to 110°F

3 cups all-purpose flour, plus more for dusting

1 tablespoon honey

¼ cup dried onion

1 teaspoon kosher salt

1 large egg, lightly beaten

1 tablespoon olive oil, for greasing

GARLIC BUTTER

4 tablespoons unsalted butter

4 cloves garlic, minced

GARNISH

1 tablespoon grated Parmesan cheese

½ teaspoon chopped fresh parsley

SPECIAL EQUIPMENT

Stand mixer

Instant-read thermometer

TO MAKE THE ROLLS:

In the bowl of a stand mixer fitted with a dough hook, sprinkle the yeast over the warm milk and let sit for 10 minutes, until foamy.

With the mixer on medium speed, add the flour, honey, dried onion, salt, and egg and mix until just combined. Increase the mixer speed to medium-high and knead for 5 minutes, until smooth and elastic.

Place the dough into a large bowl greased with the olive oil, turning to coat all over. Cover with plastic wrap and let rise for 1½ hours, until doubled in size.

Grease a 9-inch round baking pan with nonstick spray.

Punch down the dough, then turn it out onto a lightly floured surface. Cut the dough into 12 equal pieces. Place into the prepared pan. Cover with a clean kitchen towel and let rise again for 45 minutes.

Preheat the oven to 350°F.

TO MAKE THE GARLIC BUTTER:

In a small saucepan over medium heat, warm the butter and garlic. Cook for 1 to 2 minutes, until fragrant. Remove from the heat and let cool slightly. Brush the garlic mixture over the rolls, reserving a few tablespoons for later.

Bake for 22 to 25 minutes, until golden brown and an instant-read thermometer registers 190°F.

Brush the warm rolls with the reserved garlic butter.

TO GARNISH:

Sprinkle with the Parmesan cheese and parsley.

DIBS! EGG TART CUSTARD CAKE

V · PREP TIME: 25 minutes · COOK TIME: 55 minutes · YIELD: 9 servings

The Avatar shared a lot with his traveling companions: stories, games, adventures. So who could blame him if there was *one* dish in particular he wasn't as quick to split with the group? Especially when it happened to be egg tarts! This custardy cake is similar to the rich filling of Aang's most beloved snack and can be topped with Air Nomad symbols so that everyone knows who it belongs to! (You can decorate it your own way to call dibs, too!)

4 large eggs, separated

¾ cup sugar

1 cup (2 sticks) unsalted butter, melted

2 teaspoons vanilla extract

¾ cup cake flour

¼ teaspoon kosher salt

2 cups whole milk, warmed to 139°F

BLACK ROYAL ICING

2 cups powdered sugar

1 tablespoon meringue powder

2 to 3 tablespoons warm water, divided

8 drops black gel food coloring

½ teaspoon clear vanilla extract

SPECIAL EQUIPMENT

Instant-read thermometer

Stand mixer or handheld mixer

8-by-8-inch pan

Wire rack

Preheat the oven to 350°F. Line an 8-by-8-inch pan with parchment paper and coat with nonstick spray.

In the bowl of a stand mixer fitted with the whisk attachment (or in a large bowl with a handheld mixer) on medium-high speed, whip the egg whites for 4 to 5 minutes, until stiff peaks form. Set aside.

In a separate large bowl, whip the egg yolks and sugar for 3 to 5 minutes, until light and frothy. Add the butter and vanilla and beat until just combined. Slowly add the flour and salt and beat until combined. Add the milk and beat until just combined. Gently fold in the egg whites until just combined. Pour the batter into the prepared pan.

Bake for 45 to 55 minutes, until lightly browned and the custard is almost set. Let cool completely.

TO MAKE THE BLACK ROYAL ICING:

In a medium bowl with a handheld mixer on low speed, mix together the powdered sugar and meringue powder. Add half the water, the black gel food coloring, and the clear vanilla and stir until combined. Raise the speed to medium. Gradually add the remaining water as needed, and stir for 2 minutes, until thickened. Transfer to a piping bag.

Use the black icing to pipe Airbender elemental symbols on top of the cake. Cut into squares.

HEI BAI COOKIES

V · PREP TIME: 20 minutes · COOK TIME: 15 minutes · YIELD: 12 cookies

Hei Bai is a forest spirit who often takes the form of a large panda bear. Avatar Aang considered him a close personal friend, though that friendship developed *after* Aang encountered Hei Bai in his much more frightening form: as a six-limbed creature. At the time, Hei Bai was angry about the destruction of the forest outside Senlin Village . . . and had been pulling unsuspecting humans into the Spirit World. Aang was able to remind Hei Bai of nature's power to heal, and Hei Bai was able to return the villagers to their home. For those who'd already assumed that Hei Bai was a monster, the truth wasn't quite so black and white . . . but these delightful cookies made in Hei Bei's spirit form are!

COOKIES

2 cups all-purpose flour
½ teaspoon baking powder
¼ teaspoon kosher salt
6 tablespoons unsalted butter
¾ cup granulated sugar
2 large eggs
½ teaspoon vanilla extract
½ cup whole milk

ICING

2 cups powdered sugar
2 tablespoons whole milk
1 tablespoon boiling water
1 tablespoon corn syrup
¼ teaspoon kosher salt
2 tablespoons black cocoa powder

SPECIAL EQUIPMENT

Stand mixer or handheld mixer
Piping bag and small round tip
Wire rack

TO MAKE THE COOKIES:

In a medium bowl, whisk together the flour, baking powder, and salt. Set aside.

In the bowl of a stand mixer fitted with the paddle attachment (or in a large bowl with a handheld mixer) on medium speed, cream the butter and granulated sugar until combined. Add the eggs one at a time. Add the vanilla and beat until combined. Alternate adding the dry mixture and the milk and beat until just combined. Refrigerate for 15 minutes.

Preheat the oven to 350°F. Line 2 baking sheets with parchment paper.

Scoop the dough by ¼-cup portions onto the prepared baking sheets, placing them 3 inches apart.

Bake for 15 minutes, until lightly browned. Let cool on a wire rack.

TO MAKE THE ICING:

In a bowl, stir together the powdered sugar, milk, boiling water, corn syrup, and salt. Remove one-third of the icing to a small bowl and add the cocoa powder, stirring until combined.

Flip the cookies over and frost the flat sides with the white icing. Let set.

Transfer the chocolate icing to a piping bag and pipe the Hei Bai details onto the white-frosted cookies. Place cookies on a wire rack and let the icing dry.

FROZEN WOOD FROG S'MORES

PREP TIME: 1 hour, plus 5 hours freezing time · COOK TIME: 15 minutes · YIELD: 10 s'mores

Sucking on frozen frogs may not be anyone's first choice for a treat, but according to an herbalist living near the ruins of Taku, it does make a great cure for a bad cold. A far less squirmy option, these ice cream sandwiches topped with chocolate frogs are tasty anytime. They might not be the exact remedy the herbalist recommended, but at least they'll be less likely to leave a wart on your throatal flap for a month (like Sokka had to deal with after a few frozen frogs!).

CHOCOLATE FROGS

8 ounces dark chocolate, finely chopped

1 teaspoon coconut oil

1 teaspoon matcha powder

ICE CREAM–MARSHMALLOW FILLING

1 pint green tea ice cream, softened

1 pint vanilla ice cream, softened

1 cup mini marshmallows

¼ teaspoon kosher salt

GRAHAM CRACKERS

1 cup whole wheat flour

½ cup all-purpose flour, plus more for dusting

¼ cup cocoa powder

½ cup packed light brown sugar

¼ cup granulated sugar

1 teaspoon baking powder

1 teaspoon ground cinnamon

½ teaspoon kosher salt

5 tablespoons unsalted butter, softened

¼ cup honey

3 tablespoons whole milk

1 teaspoon vanilla extract

1 large egg

SPECIAL EQUIPMENT

2-inch silicone frog molds

Wire rack

TO MAKE THE CHOCOLATE FROGS:

In a microwave-safe bowl, microwave the dark chocolate for 30 seconds. Stir and microwave in 15-second increments until melted. Stir in the coconut oil until combined.

Dust the frog molds with the matcha powder. Pour in the melted chocolate. Freeze until ready to use.

TO MAKE THE ICE CREAM–MARSHMALLOW FILLING:

Line a quarter-sheet pan with parchment paper. Spread the softened green tea ice cream and vanilla ice cream into the pan. Swirl together and spread evenly. Sprinkle with the marshmallows and salt. Place in the freezer for 4 hours.

TO MAKE THE GRAHAM CRACKERS:

In a large bowl, whisk together the whole wheat flour, all-purpose flour, cocoa powder, brown sugar, granulated sugar, baking powder, cinnamon, and salt. Make a well in the center of the dry ingredients, add the butter, honey, milk, vanilla, and egg, and stir until smooth. Divide the dough in half and wrap each half in plastic wrap. Refrigerate for 1 hour.

Preheat the oven to 350°F. Line baking sheets with parchment paper.

On a floured surface, roll out the dough to 1/16 inch. Cut the dough into 2-by-5-inch rectangles. Score a line down the center. Use a fork to prick the cookies in a linear pattern. Repeat with the second dough half. Transfer the crackers to the prepared baking sheets.

Bake for 10 to 12 minutes, until just crisp. Let cool on a wire rack.

Cut the ice cream into 10 squares. Place one square on the flat side of one graham cracker. Top with a second graham cracker. Repeat with the remaining graham crackers and ice cream squares.

Remove the chocolate frogs from the molds and place one on top of each cookie sandwich. Serve before they melt!

FORTUNE TELLER PAPAYA CUPCAKES

V · PREP TIME: 20 minutes · COOK TIME: 17 minutes · YIELD: 12 cupcakes

The citizens of Makapu Village believed that fortune tellers could predict anything, from who they'd fall in love with to whether or not their village would be destroyed in a fury of volcanic doom. Katara was dismayed when Aunt Wu predicted that she'd be eating one of her least favorite fruits, papaya, for breakfast. If only she could have foreseen how delightful these papaya jam–filled cupcakes would turn out, maybe she would have embraced her fate!

CUPCAKES

1½ cups sifted cake flour
1 teaspoon baking powder
¼ teaspoon kosher salt
½ cup (1 stick) unsalted butter, softened
1 cup granulated sugar
1 tablespoon lime zest
2 large eggs
½ cup whole milk
1 tablespoon lemon juice
1 teaspoon vanilla extract
¾ cup papaya jam

FROSTING

¾ cup (1½ sticks) unsalted butter, softened
1½ cups powdered sugar
2 tablespoons papaya jam
1 teaspoon vanilla extract
¼ teaspoon kosher salt
2 tablespoons heavy whipping cream
¾ cup diced papaya

SPECIAL EQUIPMENT

Muffin pan
Cupcake liners
Wire rack
Stand mixer or handheld mixer
Piping bag and tips

Preheat the oven to 350°F. Prepare a muffin pan with liners.

TO MAKE THE CUPCAKES:
In a medium bowl, whisk together the cake flour, baking powder, and salt. Set aside.

In the bowl of a stand mixer fitted with the paddle attachment (or in a large bowl with a handheld mixer) on medium speed, cream the butter, granulated sugar, and lime zest until fluffy. Add the eggs, milk, lemon juice, and vanilla. Slowly add the dry mixture and stir until just combined. Spoon the batter into the cupcake liners.

Bake for 15 to 17 minutes, or until a toothpick inserted into the cupcakes comes out clean. Let cool on a wire rack.

Use a spoon to core out 1 tablespoon of cake from the center of each cupcake. Fill with the papaya jam. Set aside.

TO MAKE THE FROSTING:
In the bowl of a stand mixer with a whisk attachment (or in a large bowl with a handheld mixer), combine the butter, powdered sugar, papaya jam, vanilla, and salt. Add the whipping cream and whip for 1 minute, until light and fluffy.

Transfer the frosting to a piping bag fitted with a large star tip. Pipe in a circular motion on top of each cupcake. Sprinkle each with diced papaya just before serving.

STEWED SEA PRUNES PASTRY

V · PREP TIME: 15 minutes · COOK TIME: 1 hour · YIELD: 6 servings

For a member of the Southern Water Tribe, a pot of sea prunes stewing over the fire smells like *home*. But while Katara and Sokka's father, Hakoda, could've eaten a whole barrel of the things, Aang would've rather steered clear. For a fun twist on this South Pole specialty that members of any tribe will be able to enjoy, try these braided, prune-packed pastries!

FILLING

8 ounces pitted prunes

1½ cups water

½ cup granulated sugar

½ teaspoon ground cinnamon

¼ teaspoon ground cloves

½ teaspoon vanilla extract

PASTRY

One 8.5-ounce sheet puff pastry, thawed

EGG WASH

1 large egg

1 tablespoon water

ICING

½ cup powdered sugar

1 tablespoon whole milk

1 tablespoon unsalted butter, melted

SPECIAL EQUIPMENT

Immersion blender

Pastry brush

TO MAKE THE FILLING:

In a large pot, add the prunes, water, granulated sugar, cinnamon, and cloves. Bring to a boil. Lower the heat to medium-low and simmer for 30 minutes, until the water has evaporated. Let cool. Use an immersion blender to blend until smooth. Stir in the vanilla. Refrigerate until ready to use.

Preheat the oven to 375°F. Line a baking sheet with parchment paper.

TO MAKE THE PASTRY:

Place the puff pastry on the prepared baking sheet. Use the back of a knife to score the pastry width-wise into three 3-inch panels; do not cut all the way through. Spread the prune mixture across the center panel, going up to the line where the left and right panels start. Keep a 1-inch border on the top and bottom of the center panel free from the prune mixture.

With a knife, slice into the left-side panel, dividing it into eight 1-inch-wide diagonal strips that stop at the filling. The strips should remain attached to the center panel. Repeat with the right-side panel. Starting at the top of your pastry, alternate folding 1-inch strips from the left and right panels onto your center panel, over the filling. This should create a braid.

TO MAKE THE EGG WASH:

In a small bowl, whisk together the egg and water. Brush the pastry with the egg wash.

Bake for 25 to 30 minutes, until golden brown. Let cool for 5 to 10 minutes.

TO MAKE THE ICING:

In a small bowl, whisk together the powdered sugar, milk, and melted butter. Drizzle over the pastry.

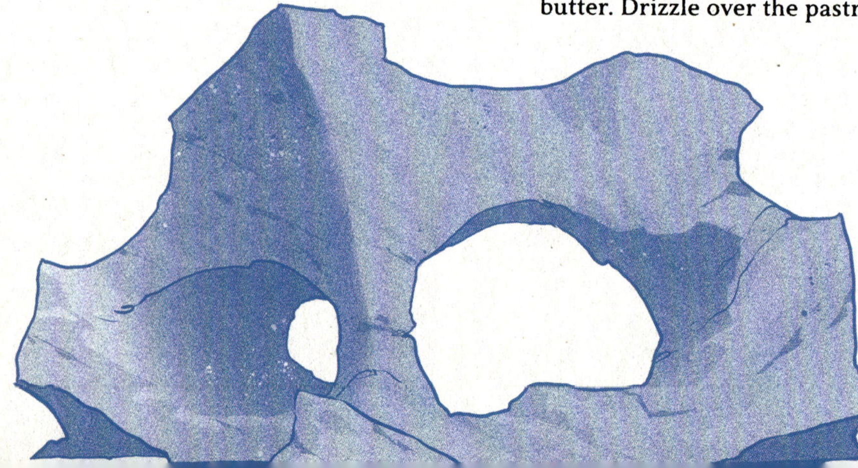

MECHANIST'S LUNCHTIME EGG PASTRIES

PREP TIME: 30 minutes · COOK TIME: 24 minutes · YIELD: 8 pastries

The mechanist living at the Northern Air Temple has a fondness for eggs. Not only does he eat them for lunch, but he has used them in his experiments (or is that eggs-periments?) as well—from testing a war balloon model to solving a gas leak. In his honor, these savory tarts, with eggs baked in a puff pastry, have all the same innovation . . . and aren't anywhere near as breakable. Enjoy them for breakfast, lunch, or any time of day!

FILLING

1 tablespoon olive oil

½ cup sliced sweet onion

4 ounces prosciutto

¼ cup crumbled feta cheese

8 medium eggs

½ teaspoon kosher salt

¼ teaspoon black pepper

1 tablespoon chopped chives, for garnish

EGG WASH

1 large egg

1 tablespoon water

PASTRY

1 package (17.3 ounces, 2 sheets) puff pastry, thawed

SPECIAL EQUIPMENT

Pastry brush

Preheat the oven to 400°F. Line a baking sheet with parchment paper.

TO MAKE THE FILLING:
In a medium skillet over medium-high heat, heat the olive oil. Add the onion and cook for 12 minutes, until caramelized. Set aside to cool.

TO MAKE THE EGG WASH:
In a small bowl, whisk together the large egg and the water.

TO MAKE THE PASTRY:
Roll out the pastry sheets to 12 inches by 12 inches, and cut each sheet into 4 equal pieces (approximately 6 inches by 6 inches), totaling 8 pieces.

Fold a pastry square into a triangle. With a sharp knife, make 2 parallel cuts ½ inch from the edges, toward the point but not touching, leaving space at the top. Unfold back into a square. Prick with a fork. Brush with the egg wash.

Take one edge and fold over to align with the inner point and press down to seal. Repeat with the opposite point, leaving the open twists intact and forming more of a diamond-shaped pastry. Brush with more egg wash, as needed. Repeat with the remaining 7 squares.

RETURNING TO THE FILLING:
Arrange the prosciutto, onions, and feta cheese around the edges of each diamond-shaped pastry, leaving a space in the center of each to crack the egg into.

Bake for 10 minutes, until the edges of your pastries begin to puff up. Remove from the oven. Use the back of a spoon to press lightly into the center of each puff pastry. Crack an egg into each one. Season with salt and pepper.

Bake for another 10 minutes, until the egg whites are set and the puff pastry is golden brown. Sprinkle with the chives.

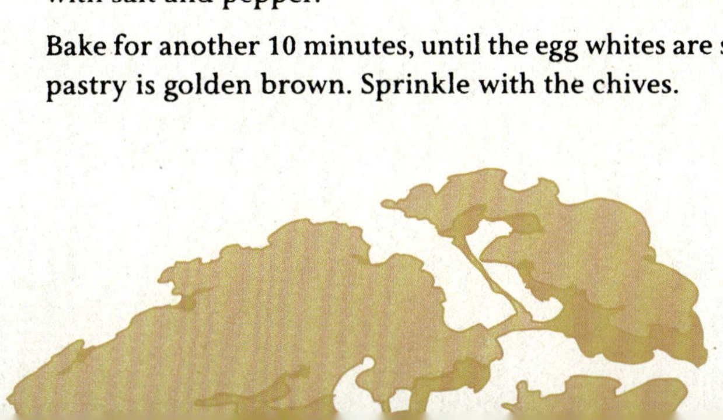

BOOK TWO

RECIPES FROM THE SECOND CHAPTER IN AVATAR AANG'S JOURNEY

In Book Two of Team Avatar's journey, Aang sought to learn more about the Avatar State—a perfect balance of body and spirit that opened up unlimited possibilities. In the stories that surround this part of Aang's adventures, he encounters different facets of bending that broaden his perspective, including the unique styles of Iroh, Toph, and Azula.

As a baker, your journey isn't all that different. Baking is about maintaining the delicate balance among ingredients, which gets easier as you learn new techniques and explore a range of flavors. The recipes in this section offer a whole lot of different flavors, from Uncle Iroh's Pai Sho Game Piece Cookies to Toph's Mud Brownies and Azula's Lightning Bolt Bites. Just remember that, Aang learned a lot from others, but mastering the Avatar State was something he had to do in his own way.

CHI TEA ENERGY BARS

GF, V, V+ · PREP TIME: 10 minutes · COOK TIME: 20 minutes · YIELD: 8 bars

Sometimes, we all need a little boost. When General Fong of the Earth Kingdom wanted Aang to transcend the physical world and tap into his spiritual energy, he served him a rare chi-enhancing tea. All that this natural stimulant ended up doing was making Aang more hyper. These matcha energy bars won't induce the Avatar State either, but they might help you "glow up" a bit in your own way.

- ½ cup peanut butter
- ¼ cup maple syrup
- 3 tablespoons packed light brown sugar
- 2 tablespoons coconut oil
- 2 cups whole rolled oats
- 1 cup puffed rice
- 1 tablespoon matcha powder
- ½ teaspoon baking soda
- ¼ teaspoon kosher salt
- ¼ cup chopped pecans
- ¼ cup golden raisins
- 2 tablespoons diced crystalized ginger
- 1 tablespoon chia seeds

SPECIAL EQUIPMENT

8-by-8-inch pan

Preheat the oven to 350°F. Line an 8 by 8 inch pan with parchment paper and coat with nonstick spray.

In a small saucepan over medium heat, add the peanut butter, maple syrup, brown sugar, and coconut oil. Cook for 1 minute, until melted. Remove from the heat.

In a large bowl, toss together the oats, puffed rice, matcha, baking soda, and salt. Pour the brown sugar mixture on top, tossing to coat. Let cool slightly. Fold in the pecans, raisins, ginger, and chia seeds. Press the mixture into the prepared pan.

Bake for 20 to 25 minutes, until lightly browned. Let cool completely in the pan. Cut into 8 equal-size bars.

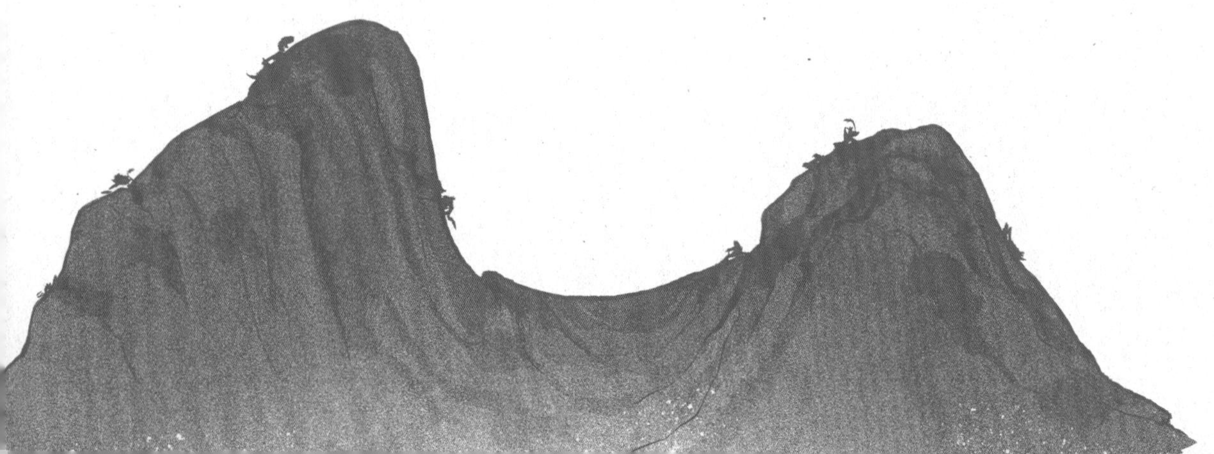

BANANA-ONION CHIPS

GF, V, V+ · PREP TIME: 20 minutes · COOK TIME: 2 hours · YIELD: 2 servings

When Aang visited Guru Pathik at the Eastern Air Temple to try to unlock the secrets of the Avatar State, he learned that he must gain balance within himself before bringing balance to the world. He also learned that onion-banana juice was an acquired taste. These chips revisit those unique ingredients, flip them a bit, and manage to bring them together harmoniously—further proof that baking, like the Avatar State, has a lot to do with *how* you approach it.

- 3 large firm bananas
- 2 tablespoons lemon juice
- 1 teaspoon kosher salt
- 1 teaspoon garlic powder
- ¼ teaspoon black pepper
- ¼ cup fried onions

SPECIAL EQUIPMENT

Wire rack

Preheat the oven to 250°F. Line a baking sheet with foil and place a wire rack on top. Coat the rack with nonstick spray.

Peel and slice the bananas into ⅛-inch-thick diagonal rounds.

In a large bowl, toss the sliced bananas with the lemon juice, salt, garlic powder, and pepper. Spread in a single layer onto the prepared wire rack.

Bake for 1 hour, flip each slice over, then bake for 1 hour longer, until dried out and crunchy. Toss with the fried onions. Serve immediately.

MIXED-UP BERRY TART

V · PREP TIME: 45 minutes, plus 2 hours 20 minutes chilling · COOK TIME: 30 minutes
YIELD: 8 servings

While on the run from Princess Azula, Prince Zuko and his uncle Iroh spent some time living off the land. This meant being careful about what they ate and drank. Some plants, like the white dragon bush, made heartbreakingly delicious tea, while others, like the white jade plant, were poisonous. Even Iroh once mixed up the two! Fortunately, bacui berries were just the cure he needed . . . though they *did* look an awful lot like maka'ole berries, which would have caused blindness instead. For the berries in this tart, we recommend picking some up at the store, where they'll be clearly labeled! (We hope.) This recipe keeps it simple with raspberries, you know, to avoid a mix-up . . .

CRUST

½ cup (1 stick) unsalted butter, softened
½ cup powdered sugar
¼ teaspoon kosher salt
1 large egg yolk
½ teaspoon almond extract
1½ cups all-purpose flour, plus more for dusting

CUSTARD

3 large egg yolks
¼ cup granulated sugar
2 tablespoons cornstarch
¼ teaspoon kosher salt
1½ cups whole milk
2 tablespoons unsalted butter, softened
1 teaspoon vanilla extract

GARNISH

3 cups raspberries
2 to 3 mint sprigs

SPECIAL EQUIPMENT

Stand mixer or handheld mixer
10-inch tart pan
Pie weights
Wire rack

TO MAKE THE CRUST:

In the bowl of a stand mixer fitted with the paddle attachment (or in a large bowl with a handheld mixer) on medium speed, cream the butter, powdered sugar, and salt until just combined. Beat in the egg yolk and almond extract until combined. Slowly add 1½ flour, beating until the dough comes together. Evenly press into a 10-inch tart pan. Refrigerate for 20 minutes.

Preheat the oven to 350°F.

Place the tart pan onto a baking sheet. Fill with pie weights.

Bake for 20 to 25 minutes, until golden brown. Let cool completely on a wire rack.

TO MAKE THE CUSTARD:

In a large bowl, whisk together the egg yolks, granulated sugar, cornstarch, and salt. Set aside.

In a large saucepan over medium-low heat, heat the milk for 2 to 3 minutes to a low simmer. Decrease the heat to low. Ladle one-third of the hot milk into the egg mixture to temper, whisking until combined.

Whisk constantly until thickened enough to coat the back of a spoon. Remove the pan from the heat. Whisk in the butter and vanilla. Remove from the heat and pour through a fine-mesh strainer set over a bowl.

Place the bowl into a larger bowl filled with ice, to create an ice bath, and let cool. Once cooled, refrigerate for 2 hours.

Carefully release the tart crust from the tart pan and place on a serving platter. Pour the cooled custard into the tart, spreading evenly with an offset spatula.

TO GARNISH:

Evenly line up the raspberries on the custard. Cover with plastic wrap and refrigerate until ready to serve. Add the mint sprigs just before serving.

ROAST DUCK BAO

PREP TIME: 3 hours, plus 8 hours chilling · COOK TIME: 2 hours 30 minutes · YIELD: 14 servings

After accidentally poisoning himself with white jade tea (see Mixed-Up Berry Tart on page 54 for *that* story), Iroh visited a hospital in an Earth Kingdom farming village, where a kind and generous young woman named Song took care of him. Song invited Iroh and Zuko to her home to enjoy a nice dinner of roast duck (which her mom always made too much of). These savory duck-filled bao buns are great to share with strangers and friends alike and nearly impossible to have too much of!

DUCK

2 pounds duck legs

1 teaspoon kosher salt

1 teaspoon ground black pepper

1 teaspoon Chinese five spice

⅓ cup chicken broth

SAUCE

½ cup apricot jam

¼ cup hoisin sauce

1 tablespoon black vinegar

1 tablespoon light brown sugar

1 tablespoon oyster sauce

1 tablespoon rice vinegar

1 teaspoon minced ginger

½ teaspoon liquid smoke

1 whole star anise

ROUX

3 tablespoons bread flour

½ cup water

TO MAKE THE DUCK:

Pat the duck legs dry. Rub the salt, pepper, and Chinese five spice all over the duck. Place on a parchment-lined baking sheet. Cover with plastic wrap. Refrigerate for 8 hours.

TO MAKE THE SAUCE:

In a medium saucepan over medium-low heat, add the apricot jam, hoisin sauce, black vinegar, brown sugar, oyster sauce, rice vinegar, ginger, liquid smoke, and star anise. Simmer for 5 minutes. Pour through a fine-mesh strainer set over a clean bowl. Let cool. Divide in half, reserving half of the sauce in the refrigerator for later.

Preheat the oven to 325°F. Coat a 13-by-9-inch pan with nonstick spray.

Place the duck legs in the prepared baking dish. Add the chicken broth. Cook for 2 hours, basting every 20 minutes. The duck is ready when an instant-read thermometer reads 165°F. Let cool slightly, then remove the meat and discard the bones. Roughly chop the meat and toss with the reserved sauce. Divide the duck into 14 portions. Refrigerate until ready to use.

TO MAKE THE ROUX:

In a saucepan over medium heat, whisk together the flour and water for 1 minute, until thickened. Turn off the heat. Transfer the roux to a bowl. Set aside to cool.

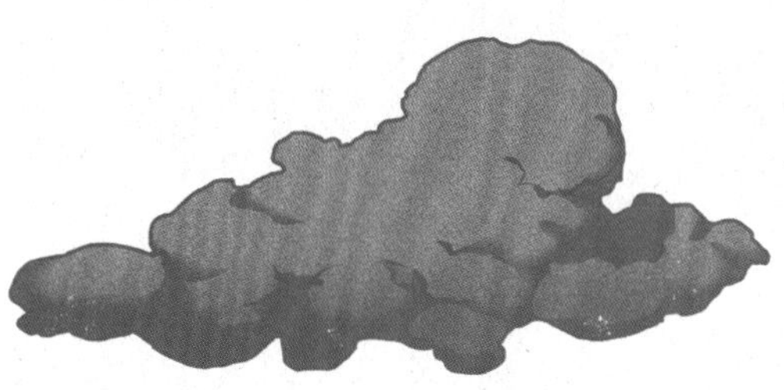

BUN DOUGH

1 envelope (2¼ teaspoons) active dry yeast

¾ cup whole milk, heated to 110°F

6 tablespoons unsalted butter, melted

3 tablespoons honey

½ teaspoon kosher salt

1 large egg, lightly beaten

3½ cups bread flour, plus more for dusting

2 tablespoons olive oil, for greasing

EGG WASH

1 egg

1 tablespoon water

1 teaspoon black sesame seeds

SIMPLE SYRUP

2 tablespoons granulated sugar

2 tablespoons boiling water

SPECIAL EQUIPMENT

Fine-mesh strainer

13-by-9-inch pan

Instant-read thermometer

Stand mixer

Pastry brush

Wire rack

TO MAKE THE BUN DOUGH:

In the bowl of a stand mixer fitted with a dough hook, sprinkle the yeast over the warm milk and let sit for 10 minutes, until foamy.

Add the butter, honey, salt, egg, and roux and mix until combined. Slowly add the flour, mixing until combined. Knead for 8 to 10 minutes until the dough is smooth and elastic.

Place the dough in a large bowl greased with the olive oil, turning to coat. Cover with plastic wrap and let rise for 1 hour, until doubled in size. Line a baking sheet with parchment paper.

Punch down the dough, then turn it out onto a floured surface. Divide into 14 equal portions and roll each into a ball. Cover the dough that you're not using with a towel. Take one ball and flatten into a flat circle. Place 2 tablespoons of the duck filling in the center, pulling up the edges and pinching to close. Place seam side down on the prepared baking sheet. Repeat with the remaining dough balls and filling. Cover with a tea towel. Let rise for 1½ hours.

Preheat the oven to 350°F.

TO MAKE THE EGG WASH:

In a small bowl, whisk together the egg and water. Brush on top of the buns. Sprinkle with the black sesame seeds.

Bake for 20 to 25 minutes, until golden brown.

TO MAKE THE SIMPLE SYRUP:

In a small bowl, stir together the granulated sugar and water until the sugar is completely dissolved. Immediately brush onto the hot buns. Let cool on a wire rack.

PENTAPOX MOCHI CAKE

GF, V · PREP TIME: 30 minutes, plus 2 hours chilling · COOK TIME: 1 hour · YIELD: 12 servings

One lesson Sokka learned up close and personal: if you get a purple pentapus stuck to your face in the sewers beneath Omashu, its strong suckers are likely to leave behind small dots that'll make people think you've caught a nasty case of pentapox. Luckily, that's not a real disease in our world . . . but this chewy mochi cake, laced with purple polka dots throughout, is as real as it gets! Thank you, sewer friend!

POLKA-DOT CAKE BALLS

8 ounces mochiko flour

1 cup sugar

1 teaspoon baking powder

¼ teaspoon kosher salt

½ cup (1 stick) unsalted butter, melted

6 ounces evaporated milk

½ teaspoon vanilla extract

2 large eggs, lightly beaten

1 teaspoon ube extract

BUNDT CAKE

16 ounces mochiko flour

2 cups sugar

2 teaspoons baking powder

½ teaspoon kosher salt

1 cup (2 sticks) unsalted butter, melted

One 12-ounce can evaporated milk

1 teaspoon clear vanilla extract

4 large eggs, lightly beaten

SPECIAL EQUIPMENT

8-by-8-inch baking pan

Instant-read thermometer

Bundt pan

Wire rack

Preheat the oven to 350°F. Line an 8-by-8-inch baking pan with parchment paper and coat with nonstick spray.

TO MAKE THE POLKA-DOT CAKE BALLS:

In a large bowl, whisk together the mochiko, sugar, baking powder, and salt. Make a well in the center of the dry ingredients and add the butter, evaporated milk, vanilla, eggs, and ube extract. Stir until combined. Pour the batter into the prepared pan.

Bake for 20 minutes, or until a toothpick inserted into the center of the cake comes out clean. Let cool completely.

Form the mixture into sixteen 2-inch balls and place on a parchment-lined baking sheet. Refrigerate for 2 hours.

TO MAKE THE BUNDT CAKE:

Preheat the oven to 350°F. Coat a Bundt pan with nonstick spray.

In a large bowl, whisk together the mochiko, sugar, baking powder, and salt. Make a well in the center of the dry ingredients and add the butter, evaporated milk, clear vanilla, and eggs. Stir until combined.

Pour one-third of the batter into the prepared Bundt pan. Add half the polka-dot cake balls. Pour over another one-third of the batter, and then add a second layer of cake balls. Finally, pour over the remaining batter.

Place the Bundt pan on a baking sheet and bake for 1 hour, until the internal temperature reads 200°F on an instant-read thermometer. Let cool completely, then turn out onto a wire rack.

NEW OZAI BERRY BARS

V · PREP TIME: 20 minutes · COOK TIME: 35 minutes · YIELD: 12 bars

Momo loves to snack, but this little lemur's big appetite often gets him into even bigger trouble. One time, he swooped through a window in New Ozai—the city formerly known as Omashu—to nibble on a bowl of berries and somehow ended up kidnapping the governor's infant son! If Team Avatar had some of these berry crumble bars on hand that day, it might've saved everyone a lot of trouble!

CRUST

2 cups all-purpose flour

½ cup powdered sugar

¾ cup (1½ sticks) unsalted butter, softened

FILLING

3 cups blueberries

2 cups blackberries

2 cups raspberries

2 tablespoons unsalted butter, melted

¼ cup packed light brown sugar

½ teaspoon vanilla extract

½ teaspoon ground cinnamon

¼ teaspoon ground nutmeg

¼ teaspoon kosher salt

TOPPING

½ cup (1 stick) cold unsalted butter, cubed

1 cup rolled oats

¾ cup all-purpose flour

¾ cup packed light brown sugar

1 teaspoon ground cinnamon

¼ teaspoon kosher salt

SPECIAL EQUIPMENT

13-by-9-inch pan

Stand mixer or handheld mixer

Preheat the oven to 350°F. Line a 13-by-9-inch pan with parchment paper and coat with nonstick spray.

TO MAKE THE CRUST:
In the bowl of a stand mixer fitted with the paddle attachment (or in a large bowl with a handheld mixer) on medium speed, beat the flour, powdered sugar, and butter until just combined. Press into the prepared pan. Prick lightly with a fork.

Bake for 10 minutes. Set aside to cool slightly.

TO MAKE THE FILLING:
In a large bowl, combine the blueberries, blackberries, raspberries, melted butter, brown sugar, vanilla, cinnamon, nutmeg, and salt. Spoon over the baked crust.

TO MAKE THE TOPPING:
In a small bowl, cut together the butter, oats, flour, brown sugar, cinnamon, and salt. Crumble on top of the fruit mixture.

Bake for 25 minutes, until browned. Let cool. Cut into 12 bars.

UNFRIED DOUGH PIE

V · PREP TIME: 3 hours, plus 30 minutes chilling time · COOK TIME: 1 hour 40 minutes
YIELD: 8 servings

Want a great way to celebrate the day that the Avatar was *not* boiled in oil by the people of Chin Village? No need to throw a huge festival in his honor. Instead, show your appreciation by baking this special New Avatar Day pie, with a crust made from a latticework of tiny dough Aangs meant to look like a certain bowl of Avatars presented to our heroes after their victory. Its unfried goodness offers a nice break from Sokka's favorite deep-fried festival foods.

CRUST

4 cups all-purpose flour, plus more for dusting

1 tablespoon granulated sugar

1 teaspoon kosher salt

1½ cups (3 sticks) cold unsalted butter, cubed

½ cup ice water

2 drops light blue gel food coloring, for decorating

Coat a 9-inch pie plate with nonstick spray. Line a baking sheet with parchment paper.

TO MAKE THE CRUST:

In a large bowl, whisk together the flour, granulated sugar, and salt. Using a pastry cutter, cut the cold butter into the flour mixture until crumbly. Add the ice water, 1 tablespoon at a time, mixing until the dough just comes together. Divide the dough in half and pat into disks. Wrap each disk in plastic wrap and refrigerate for 30 minutes.

On a lightly floured surface, roll out one pie dough disk into a 15-inch circle. Transfer to the prepared pie plate, pressing into the bottom and up the sides. Refrigerate until ready to use.

On the same floured surface, roll out the second dough disk to ¼ inch thick. Use a cutter to cut out 24 Avatar-shaped pieces. Place on the prepared baking sheet.

Use a kitchen paintbrush and light blue gel food coloring to paint an arrow on each Avatar head. Then use a toothpick to create the eyes. Place the dough cutouts in the refrigerator until ready to use.

CARAMEL SAUCE

1 cup granulated sugar

¼ cup water

6 tablespoons unsalted butter, cubed

½ cup heavy cream

1 teaspoon vanilla extract

FILLING

8 large Granny Smith apples (about 3 pounds)

2 tablespoons lemon juice

½ cup cornstarch

½ cup granulated sugar

¼ cup packed light brown sugar

1 tablespoon ground cinnamon

1 teaspoon ground nutmeg

½ teaspoon kosher salt

4 tablespoons cold unsalted butter, cubed

TO MAKE THE CARAMEL SAUCE:

In a small saucepan over medium heat, heat the granulated sugar and water until the sugar melts and turns a golden brown, about 10 minutes. Add the butter and whisk until just combined. Remove from the heat and whisk in the heavy cream. Place back on the heat and cook for 1 minute more, until bubbly. Turn off the heat and stir in the vanilla. Let cool.

Preheat the oven to 400°F.

TO MAKE THE FILLING:

Peel and core the apples. Cut into ¼-inch-thick slices.

In a large bowl, toss the apples with the lemon juice. Add the cornstarch, granulated sugar, brown sugar, cinnamon, nutmeg, and salt, tossing to coat.

Remove the pie plate from the refrigerator. Layer one-fourth of the apples in the plate. Dot with one-third of the cubed butter. Pour over one-third of the caramel sauce. Repeat this process with the apples, butter, and caramel sauce two more times. Then top with the remaining one-fourth of the apples. Arrange the Avatar cutouts over the filling to create a top crust, leaving openings for venting.

EGG WASH

1 large egg

1 tablespoon water

1 tablespoon coarse sanding sugar, for sprinkling

SPECIAL EQUIPMENT

9-inch pie plate

Pastry cutter

5-inch person-shaped cookie cutter

Kitchen paintbrush

Pastry brush

TO MAKE THE EGG WASH:

In a small bowl, whisk together the egg and water. Brush onto the Avatar cutout crust. Sprinkle with the sanding sugar.

Bake for 15 minutes, then add a foil tent to the top of the pie. Lower the oven temperature to 350°F. Continue baking for 1 hour. Remove the foil tent and bake for an additional 15 minutes, until golden brown. Let cool completely.

POSSUM-CHICKEN PIES

PREP TIME: 20 minutes · COOK TIME: 20 minutes · YIELD: 12 pies

The Earth Kingdom's Foggy Swamp was full of lush vegetation, unique animals, and a tribe of Waterbenders who used their powers in unusual ways. Though they pursued all types of creatures (including Momo!), the staple of their diet was possum-chicken. Next time the swamp is calling you, bake up this chicken wrapped in puff pastry. We assume it tastes just like possum-chicken (which, according to Sokka, tastes just like arctic hen).

FILLING

1 tablespoon olive oil

1 shallot, minced

2 cloves garlic, minced

1 teaspoon minced fresh ginger

2 cups diced roasted chicken

½ cup chicken broth

1 tablespoon curry powder

1 teaspoon ground cumin

1 teaspoon ground turmeric

½ teaspoon allspice

½ teaspoon kosher salt

¼ teaspoon black pepper

CRUST

1 package (17.3 ounces, 2 sheets) puff pastry, thawed

EGG WASH

2 large eggs

2 tablespoons water

SPECIAL EQUIPMENT

Pastry brush

TO MAKE THE FILLING:

In a skillet over medium-high heat, heat the olive oil. Add the shallot, garlic, and ginger and cook for 3 to 4 minutes, until softened. Add the chicken, chicken broth, curry powder, cumin, turmeric, allspice, salt, and pepper. Simmer for 5 to 7 minutes, until fragrant and slightly thickened. Let cool.

Preheat the oven to 400°F. Line a baking sheet with parchment paper.

TO MAKE THE CRUST:

Roll out the pastry sheets to 12 inches by 12 inches, and cut each sheet into 6 equal pieces (approximately 6 inches by 4 inches), totaling 12 pieces.

TO MAKE THE EGG WASH:

In a small bowl, whisk together the eggs and water. Brush a small amount of egg wash on all four edges of a pastry square.

Add 2 tablespoons of filling in the center of a pastry square and fold one side over, creating a rectangle. Use a fork to crimp the edges. Place on the prepared baking sheet. Repeat with the remaining pastry squares and filling.

Brush the remaining egg wash on all of the filled pies. Bake for 18 to 20 minutes, until golden brown. Let cool slightly.

APPA BAKED BRIE

GF · PREP TIME: 20 minutes · COOK TIME: 45 minutes · YIELD: 8 servings

At first, Appa seems intimidating to people like Sokka who have never seen a real sky bison before. But once Sokka got to know the big guy, he realized that Appa was all soft and gooey on the inside . . . sort of like this baked Brie. This melty mountain is more than enough to share with your entire team (assuming no one has five stomachs like Appa). It'll have everyone shouting, "Yip Yip!"

BACON

3 slices thick-cut bacon

1 tablespoon light brown sugar

¼ teaspoon black pepper

¼ teaspoon smoked paprika

¼ teaspoon cayenne pepper

APPLES

1 tablespoon unsalted butter

1 Granny Smith apple, cored and sliced

1 tablespoon light brown sugar

¼ teaspoon ground cinnamon

¼ teaspoon kosher salt

BRIE

One 1-pound Brie wheel

2 whole dried cranberries

FOR SERVING

Sliced sourdough

SPECIAL EQUIPMENT

Wire rack

Preheat the oven to 375°F. Line a baking sheet with foil and place a wire rack on top. Coat the rack with nonstick spray.

TO MAKE THE BACON:

Sprinkle both sides of the bacon slices with the brown sugar, black pepper, paprika, and cayenne pepper. Place on the prepped rack.

Bake for 17 to 20 minutes, until browned. Let cool for 2 to 3 minutes. Reserve 2 bacon strips as is. Crumble the third. Set aside.

TO MAKE THE APPLES:

In a large skillet over medium-high heat, melt the butter. Add the sliced apples, brown sugar, cinnamon, and salt. Cook for 6 to 9 minutes, until the apples have softened. Set aside.

Preheat the oven to 350°F. Line a baking dish with parchment paper.

TO MAKE THE BRIE:

Place the Brie in the prepared baking dish. Use a knife to score the top. Bake for 15 minutes, until softened.

Use the cooked apples to create Appa's arrow and face on the Brie. Add the crumbled bacon for his nose. Use the whole bacon strips, one on each side of his head, to create his horns. Place the dried cranberries to create Appa's eyes.

Decorate the baking dish with the remaining cooked apples, bacon, and sourdough bread. Serve immediately.

APPA MACAROONS

V · PREP TIME: 1 hour · COOK TIME: 30 minutes · YIELD: 8 macaroons

The beauty of spring. Leaves grow on trees, flowers bloom, and Appa gets a new coat. Unfortunately, that also meant he leaves huge wads of fur everywhere! Or, as Ty Lee once said, "Not wads. They're more like bundles. Or bunches? Clumps! They're clumps!" The shredded coconut in these mound cookies won't make a great wig or fake beard, but it will give these mini-Appas their signature shaggy coat—while hopefully causing significantly less sneezing!

COOKIE DOUGH

1½ cups all-purpose flour, plus more for dusting

½ teaspoon baking powder

¼ teaspoon kosher salt

½ cup (1 stick) unsalted butter, softened

½ cup granulated sugar

1 large egg

½ teaspoon vanilla extract

2 drops black gel food coloring

MACAROONS

14 ounces sweetened flaked coconut

1 cup sweetened condensed milk

1 teaspoon almond extract

¼ teaspoon kosher salt

2 large egg whites

BLACK ROYAL ICING

1 cup powdered sugar

1 teaspoon meringue powder

1 to 2 tablespoons warm water

4 drops black gel food coloring

¼ teaspoon clear vanilla extract

Preheat the oven to 350°F. Line 1 small baking sheet with parchment paper.

TO MAKE THE COOKIE DOUGH:

In a medium bowl, whisk together the 1½ cups flour, baking powder, and salt. Set aside.

In the bowl of a stand mixer fitted with the paddle attachment (or in a large bowl with a handheld mixer) on medium speed, cream the butter and granulated sugar until combined. Add the egg, vanilla, and black gel food coloring and mix until just combined. Add the flour mixture and beat until just combined. Wrap the dough in plastic wrap. Refrigerate for 20 minutes.

On a lightly floured surface, roll out the dough to ¼ inch thick. Cut out 3-inch ovals (these will be Appa's face on each macaroon) and 3-inch arrows (these will go atop his head), making 8 of each. Set aside in the refrigerator to be baked later.

Take ¼ teaspoon of the remaining cookie dough and roll into a 3-inch-long horn. Repeat to make 16 horns total. Place on the small prepared baking sheet. Bake for 5 to 7 minutes, until lightly browned. Let cool on a wire rack.

Line an additional 2 baking sheets with parchment paper.

TO MAKE THE MACAROONS:

In a large bowl, combine the coconut, sweetened condensed milk, almond extract, and salt. Set aside.

In the bowl of a stand mixer fitted with the whisk attachment (or in a large bowl with a handheld mixer) on medium speed, whip the egg whites until stiff peaks form. Fold the egg whites into the coconut mixture.

Scoop the batter into 8 balls and place on the prepared baking sheets. Flatten each slightly. Bake for 15 minutes. Remove from the oven.

TO ASSEMBLE:

Add one refrigerated cookie dough oval to the center of each macaroon. Then, place one refrigerated cookie dough arrow at the top of each macaroon. Return the macaroons to the oven. Bake for an additional 10 minutes, until the coconut and the cookie pieces are browned. Let sit on the trays for 15 minutes before moving to cool on a wire rack.

DECORATION

12 large pink heart sprinkles

SPECIAL EQUIPMENT

Stand mixer or handheld mixer

Wire rack

Piping bag and tips

TO MAKE THE BLACK ROYAL ICING:

In a medium bowl with a handheld mixer on low speed, mix together the powdered sugar and meringue powder. Add half the water, the black gel food coloring, and the clear vanilla and mix until combined. Raise the speed to medium. Gradually add the remaining water as needed, and mix for 2 minutes, until thickened. Transfer to a piping bag.

TO DECORATE:

Once the Appa macaroons have cooled, use the black icing to pipe Appa's eyes and nose onto the oval cookie faces. Use some of the icing to adhere the horns and an upside-down heart sprinkle, for his tongue, to each.

AZULA'S LIGHTNING BOLT BITES

V · PREP TIME: 30 minutes · COOK TIME: 30 minutes · YIELD: 10 scones

Some of the most powerful Firebenders can use their abilities to redirect lightning. Uncle Iroh claimed that this was a pure expression of firebending, one that was without aggression and not fueled by rage or emotion. His niece, Princess Azula, may not have agreed. These savory lightning bolt scones capture the "cold-blooded fire" in baked form, packed with flavor as jolting as Azula's temper.

2 tablespoons olive oil

1 tablespoon minced shallot

1 cup diced red onion

¼ teaspoon black pepper

2½ cups all-purpose flour, plus more for dusting

1 tablespoon baking powder

½ teaspoon garlic powder

½ teaspoon kosher salt

¼ teaspoon chili powder

¼ teaspoon smoked paprika

½ cup (1 stick) cold unsalted butter, cubed

½ cup buttermilk

2 tablespoons gochujang

1 large egg, lightly beaten

1½ cups shredded cheddar cheese

¼ cup diced green onion

¼ cup heavy cream

SPECIAL EQUIPMENT

Wire rack

In a large skillet over medium-high heat, heat the olive oil. Add the shallot and cook for 2 to 3 minutes, until softened. Add the red onion and cook for 12 to 15 minutes, until browned and caramelized. Season with black pepper. Set aside to cool.

Preheat the oven to 375°F. Line a baking sheet with parchment paper.

In a large bowl, whisk together the flour, baking powder, garlic powder, salt, chili powder, and paprika. Cut the butter into the dry ingredients, until crumbly. Stir in the buttermilk, gochujang, and egg until just combined. Fold in the cooled cooked onion, cheese, and green onion.

On a lightly floured surface, pat out the dough to ¾ inch thick. Cut out lightning bolt shapes, then transfer to the prepared baking sheet. Brush the tops with the heavy cream.

Bake for 18 to 20 minutes, until golden brown. Let cool on a wire rack.

AIRBENDER STAFFS

V · PREP TIME: 1 hour · COOK TIME: 50 minutes · YIELD: 24 pretzels

When master Earthbender Toph Beifong first joined Team Avatar, her pragmatic approach took a little time for Aang, Katara, and Sokka to get used to. It wasn't all smooth sailing . . . or gliding. Especially not when she used Aang's antique glider staff—a delicate instrument made by the monks—as a nutcracker! It may not have thrilled Aang, but it did inspire these tasty chocolate-dipped, nut-covered pretzel sticks.

PRETZELS

1 envelope (2¼ teaspoons) active dry yeast

1 cup water, heated to 110°F

2 cups all-purpose flour

1 cup bread flour

2 teaspoons light brown sugar

¼ teaspoon kosher salt

1 tablespoon olive oil, for greasing

8 cups water

½ cup baking soda

EGG WASH

1 large egg

1 tablespoon water

1 tablespoon kosher salt

COATING

20 ounces caramels

3 tablespoons heavy cream

16 ounces dark chocolate, finely chopped

1 tablespoon coconut oil

1½ cups chopped pecans

SPECIAL EQUIPMENT

Stand mixer

Pastry brush

Wire rack

Double boiler

Line baking sheets with parchment paper.

TO MAKE THE PRETZELS:

In the bowl of a stand mixer fitted with a dough hook, sprinkle the yeast over the warm water and let sit for 5 minutes, until foamy.

With the mixer on medium, add the all-purpose flour, bread flour, brown sugar, and salt and mix until just combined. Increase the mixer speed to medium-high and knead for 5 minutes, until smooth and elastic. Place the dough in a large bowl greased with oil, turning to coat. Cover with plastic wrap and let rise for 30 to 35 minutes.

Cut the dough into 24 equal pieces. Roll out one piece into a thin rod approximately 12 inches long. Place on the prepared baking sheet. Repeat with the remaining pieces. Cover with a towel and let rise for 10 minutes.

In a large pot, bring the water to a boil. Add the baking soda.

Add 2 or 3 pretzel rods to the pot, boil for 10 seconds, then transfer to a prepared baking sheet.

Preheat the oven to 350°F.

TO MAKE THE EGG WASH:

In a small bowl, whisk together the egg and water. Brush each pretzel rod with the egg wash and sprinkle with the salt.

Bake for 30 minutes, until dark brown in color. Let cool completely on a wire rack.

Lay out parchment paper and coat with nonstick spray. Set aside.

TO MAKE THE COATING:

In a microwave-safe bowl, melt the caramels and heavy cream for 30 seconds on high, then at 15-second intervals until smooth. Dip the pretzels into the caramel and place on the prepared parchment paper.

To the base of a double boiler add 2 inches of water. Bring to a low simmer over medium heat. Place the top part of the double boiler over the water. Add the dark chocolate. Stir until melted. Stir in the coconut oil.

Drizzle the melted chocolate over the caramel-coated pretzels. Sprinkle with the chopped pecans. Let the chocolate set.

MISTY PALMS MANGO SHORTCAKE

V · PREP TIME: 35 minutes · COOK TIME: 15 minutes · YIELD: 8 shortcakes

When the members of Team Avatar each picked mini-vacations to go on, Katara thought Misty Palms Oasis sounded like a perfect spot. Sadly, this pristine natural ice spring, formerly one of nature's wonders, must've changed ownership since Aang's last visit. Though the ice was mostly gone, this desert town still served chilled beverages made from mango and other freshly chopped fruits. This Misty Palms–inspired mango shortcake is like a vacation in your mouth, a great reward when you've been training your arrow off!

MANGO TOPPING

4 cups cubed mango

½ cup honey

¼ teaspoon kosher salt

WHIPPED CREAM

1½ cups heavy whipping cream

3 tablespoons powdered sugar

1 teaspoon vanilla extract

BISCUITS

2 cups self-rising flour, plus more for dusting

¼ cup granulated sugar

½ teaspoon ground cinnamon

¼ teaspoon ground nutmeg

¼ teaspoon kosher salt

½ cup (1 stick) cold unsalted butter, cubed

¾ cup buttermilk

¼ cup heavy cream

1 teaspoon coarse sanding sugar

SPECIAL EQUIPMENT

Stand mixer or handheld mixer

Pastry cutter

3-inch biscuit cutter

Wire rack

TO MAKE THE MANGO TOPPING:

In a large bowl, toss the mango, honey, and salt. Refrigerate until ready to use.

TO MAKE THE WHIPPED CREAM:

In the bowl of a stand mixer fitted with the whisk attachment (or in a large bowl with a handheld mixer) on medium speed, whip the cream, powdered sugar, and vanilla for 5 to 7 minutes, until soft peaks form. Place in the refrigerator until ready to use.

Preheat the oven to 400°F. Line a baking sheet with parchment paper.

TO MAKE THE BISCUITS:

In a large bowl, whisk together the self-rising flour, granulated sugar, cinnamon, nutmeg, and salt. Use a pastry cutter to cut in the butter until crumbly. Work in the buttermilk until just combined.

Turn out onto a lightly floured surface. Knead lightly. Pat out to 1 inch thick. Use a 3-inch round cutter to cut out 8 biscuits. Transfer to the prepared baking sheet. Brush with the heavy cream and sprinkle with the coarse sanding sugar.

Bake for 18 to 20 minutes, until golden brown. Transfer to a wire rack to cool.

TO ASSEMBLE THE SHORTCAKES:

Cut each biscuit in half horizontally. On the bottom half, layer on the mango topping and whipped cream, then add the top half.

TOPH'S MUD BROWNIES

V · PREP TIME: 20 minutes · COOK TIME: 40 minutes · YIELD: 9 brownies

When they became lost in the Si Wong Desert after visiting Wan Shi Tong's lost library, a dehydrated Toph said that her mouth may have tasted like mud the day before, but now it just tasted like sand. She never thought she'd miss the taste of mud so much. These rich, chocolaty brownies only *look* like mud, but you'll be missing their taste as soon as they're gone too!

1 cup all-purpose flour
½ cup packed light brown sugar
½ cup granulated sugar
¼ cup unsweetened cocoa powder
¼ teaspoon kosher salt
¼ cup brewed coffee, cooled
¼ cup vegetable oil
2 large eggs, lightly beaten
1 teaspoon vanilla extract
2 tablespoons unsalted butter, melted
2 ounces dark chocolate, melted
1 cup semisweet chocolate chunks

SPECIAL EQUIPMENT
8-by-8-inch pan

Preheat the oven to 350°F. Line an 8-by-8-inch baking pan with parchment paper and coat with nonstick spray.

In a large bowl, whisk together the flour, brown sugar, granulated sugar, cocoa powder, and salt. Make a well in the center of the dry ingredients and pour in the coffee, oil, eggs, and vanilla. Stir until combined. Fold in the melted butter and melted chocolate, then fold in the chocolate chunks. Pour the batter into the prepared pan.

Bake for 30 minutes, until just set. Let cool completely. Cut into squares.

UNCLE IROH'S PAI SHO GAME PIECE COOKIES

V · PREP TIME: 15 minutes · COOK TIME: 17 minutes · YIELD: 12 cookies

Uncle Iroh loved a game of Pai Sho almost as much as he loved tea. It was said that those who clung to the game's ancient ways could always find a friend. Offer to share a batch of these almond cookies shaped like Pai Sho tiles, and we wager you'll find friends too! Just make sure to save some for yourself, so you're not the unlucky soul who has an incomplete Pai Sho set!

2¼ cups all-purpose flour

½ teaspoon baking soda

½ teaspoon ground cinnamon

¼ teaspoon kosher salt

½ cup sugar

½ cup (1 stick) unsalted butter

1 teaspoon almond extract

½ cup vegetable oil

½ cup sliced almonds

SPECIAL EQUIPMENT

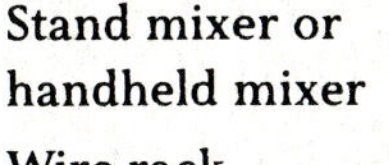

Stand mixer or handheld mixer

Wire rack

Preheat the oven to 325°F. Line a baking sheet with parchment paper.

In a medium bowl, whisk together the flour, baking soda, cinnamon, and salt. Set aside.

In the bowl of a stand mixer fitted with the paddle attachment (or in a large bowl with a handheld mixer) on medium speed, cream the sugar and butter until fluffy. Stir in the almond extract. Alternate stirring in the dry mixture with the vegetable oil, adding both in phases and stirring until just combined.

Form the dough into twelve 2½-inch balls. Flatten each and top with the almond slices, arranged to look like Pai Sho game pieces.

Bake for 15 to 17 minutes, until lightly browned. Let cool on a wire rack.

JASMINE TEA CAKE ROLL

V · PREP TIME: 30 minutes, plus 30 minutes cooling and 1 hour chilling time · COOK TIME: 15 minutes · YIELD: 8 servings

Shortly after Iroh and Zuko arrived in the Earth Kingdom's capital city, Iroh ordered jasmine tea from a vendor who claimed to sell the finest tea in Ba Sing Se. When it turned out to be the coldest tea in Ba Sing Se, Iroh thought it was a disgrace. But this tea-infused Swiss roll cake filled with cooled cream proves that there's no reason to cry over chilled tea.

CAKE

3 large eggs, separated
4 tablespoons granulated sugar, divided
¼ cup whole milk
2 tablespoons canola oil
½ teaspoon vanilla extract
⅓ cup cake flour
1 tablespoon finely ground jasmine tea leaves
½ teaspoon baking powder
¼ teaspoon kosher salt
½ teaspoon cream of tartar

FILLING

1 cup whipping cream
⅓ cup powdered sugar
⅓ cup lemon curd

DECORATION

¼ cup fresh raspberries
Mint leaves
1 tablespoon powdered sugar, plus more for dusting

SPECIAL EQUIPMENT

13-by-9-inch pan
Stand mixer or handheld mixer
Offset spatula
Piping bag with a star tip

Preheat the oven to 325°F. Line a 13-by-9-inch pan with parchment paper and coat with nonstick spray.

TO MAKE THE CAKE:

In a large bowl, mix the egg yolks and 2 tablespoons of the sugar until pale in color. Stir in the milk, oil, and vanilla. Stir in the cake flour, jasmine tea leaves, baking powder, and salt until just combined. Set aside.

In the bowl of a stand mixer fitted with the whisk attachment (or in a large bowl with a handheld mixer) on medium-high speed, whip the egg whites until frothy. Slowly add in the remaining 2 tablespoons of sugar and the cream of tartar, whipping until stiff peaks form. Gently fold the whipped egg whites into the egg yolk mixture until just combined. Pour the batter into the prepared pan, spreading evenly with an offset spatula. Tap the pan on the counter to release air.

Bake for 15 minutes, until a toothpick inserted into the center of the cake comes out clean. Cool for 5 minutes.

Dust a clean kitchen towel with powdered sugar. Turn the warm cake out onto the towel. Peel off the parchment paper. Roll the cake up along the short edge, along with the towel. Let cool in the rolled-up towel for 20 to 30 minutes.

TO MAKE THE FILLING:

In the bowl of a stand mixer fitted with the whisk attachment (or in a large bowl with a handheld mixer) on medium-high speed, whip the cream and powdered sugar for 2 to 3 minutes, until stiff peaks form. Reserve ½ cup of the whipped cream for decorating, refrigerating until ready to use.

Gently unroll the cake from the towel. Evenly spread the lemon curd onto the cake, leaving a 1-inch border at the end of the cake. Top with the whipped cream. Slowly roll the cake back up, along the same seamline. Transfer to a serving plate, seam side down. Cover with plastic wrap and refrigerate for 1 hour.

Slice the two short ends off of the cake log to create clean edges.

TO DECORATE THE CAKE:

Place the reserved whipped cream into a piping bag fitted with a star tip. Decorate the top of the cake with bursts of whipped cream. Add raspberries and mint leaves to garnish. Dust with powdered sugar just before serving.

KILLER SHRIMP TOAST

PREP TIME: 10 minutes · COOK TIME: 25 minutes · YIELD: 8 pieces

Sokka couldn't help but wonder what strange challenges awaited Team Avatar inside Ba Sing Se's inner walls. He even worried that the city might've been submerged in an ocean full of killer shrimp! Sure, it sounded like he'd been hitting the cactus juice again, but to be fair, weird stuff happened to them all the time. And at least his wild imagination inspired this totally killer shrimp toast!

8 ounces raw shrimp, peeled and deveined
1 large egg, lightly beaten
2 green onions, minced
2 cloves garlic, minced
1 teaspoon minced ginger
1 tablespoon chili crisp
1 tablespoon cornstarch
1 teaspoon soy sauce
1 teaspoon sesame oil
¼ teaspoon black pepper
¼ teaspoon kosher salt
4 slices white sandwich bread
2 tablespoons black sesame seeds
2 tablespoons white sesame seeds
1 tablespoon chopped cilantro, for garnish

Preheat the oven to 400°F. Line a baking sheet with parchment paper.

Finely mince the shrimp. In a large bowl, stir together the minced shrimp, egg, green onions, garlic, ginger, chili crisp, cornstarch, soy sauce, sesame oil, pepper, and salt until well combined. Set aside.

Cut the crusts off the sandwich bread slices, then cut each slice into 2 triangles. Spread the shrimp mixture onto the triangles.

In a flat dish, stir together the black and white sesame seeds. Dip the shrimp-coated bread triangles into the sesame seeds. Place on the prepared baking sheet.

Bake for 10 to 12 minutes, until golden brown. Sprinkle with the cilantro. Serve immediately.

HOT LEAF JUICE CAKE

V · PREP TIME: 2 hours 20 minutes, plus chilling overnight
COOK TIME: 1 hour 45 minutes · YIELD: 10 servings

To Iroh, being sick of tea was like being sick of breathing. But Zuko claimed that his uncle's favorite beverage was nothing more than hot leaf juice. If only Zuko had tried this cheesecake, he might not have said something so horrible . . . and horribly untrue! The secret ingredient here isn't love, it's the powdered green tea known as matcha. (Okay, it's also love.) Sharing this dessert with a fascinating stranger is one of life's true delights.

CRUST

1½ cups graham cracker crumbs

6 tablespoons unsalted butter, melted

¼ teaspoon kosher salt

CHEESECAKE

24 ounces cream cheese, softened

2 cups granulated sugar

3 tablespoons cornstarch

1 tablespoon lemon juice

1 tablespoon vanilla extract

¼ teaspoon kosher salt

6 large eggs, at room temperature

¾ cup sour cream

1 tablespoon matcha powder

TOPPING

2 tablespoons matcha powder

1 tablespoon powdered sugar

SPECIAL EQUIPMENT

9-inch springform pan

Stand mixer or handheld mixer

Wire rack

Large roasting pan

Preheat the oven to 350°F. Wrap a 9-inch springform pan with heavy-duty aluminum foil.

TO MAKE THE CRUST:

In a medium bowl, stir the graham cracker crumbs, butter, and salt until combined. Press the mixture into the bottom of the prepared pan.

Bake the crust for 10 to 12 minutes, until lightly browned. Let cool completely.

Decrease the oven temperature to 300°F.

TO MAKE THE CHEESECAKE:

In the bowl of a stand mixer fitted with the paddle attachment (or in a large bowl with a handheld mixer) on medium speed, cream the cream cheese, granulated sugar, cornstarch, lemon juice, vanilla, and salt until just combined.

Decrease the speed to low and add the eggs one at a time. Add the sour cream and beat until just combined but the batter is smooth.

Divide the batter equally between 2 bowls. Stir the matcha powder into one bowl until combined.

Place the wrapped springform pan into a large roasting pan. Add one-fourth of the white batter on top of the crust, followed by one-fourth of the matcha batter, alternating until the all the batter has been used.

Make a water bath by pouring boiling water into the roasting pan up to 1 inch on the side of the springform pan. Bake for 1 hour and 30 minutes, until the cake is just set and slightly wobbly. Remove the roasting pan from the oven, leaving the cheesecake in the water bath untouched for 1 hour.

Remove the springform pan from the water bath and run a knife around the edge of the cake to loosen it from the edge. Discard the foil. Cover with plastic wrap and place the refrigerator to cool overnight.

Release the springform pan and removing the ring.

TO MAKE THE TOPPING:

Dust the top with sifted matcha powder and powdered sugar.

LAVENDER LEMON BARS

V · PREP TIME: 30 minutes · COOK TIME: 50 minutes · YIELD: 18 bars

A picnic is a perfect way to spend any day, but it can be an especially peaceful way to spend a moment of remembrance. To commemorate his late son Lu Ten's birthday, Iroh bought a lovely lavender picnic basket from a vendor in Ba Sing Se. These lemon bars, made with a hint of lavender, pay homage to this tender moment.

LAVENDER SUGAR

1½ cups granulated sugar

1 teaspoon dried lavender

CRUST

2 cups all-purpose flour

½ cup powdered sugar

½ teaspoon kosher salt

1 cup (2 sticks) cold unsalted butter, cubed

FILLING

6 large eggs

1½ cups lavender sugar (above)

⅔ cup fresh lemon juice

¼ cup fresh lime juice

1 tablespoon lemon zest

½ cup all-purpose flour

½ teaspoon dried lavender

TOPPING

¼ cup powdered sugar

1 teaspoon dried lavender

SPECIAL EQUIPMENT

Food processor

13-by-9-inch pan

Pastry cutter

Stand mixer or handheld mixer

TO MAKE THE LAVENDER SUGAR:

In a food processor, blend ½ cup of the sugar and the dried lavender. Stir together with the remaining 1 cup of sugar. Set aside.

Preheat the oven to 350°F. Coat a 13-by-9-inch pan with nonstick spray.

TO MAKE THE CRUST:

In a large bowl, whisk together the flour, powdered sugar, and salt. Use a pastry cutter to cut in the butter until crumbly. Press the crust into the prepped pan close to the edges. Bake for 20 minutes, until lightly golden. Set aside.

TO MAKE THE FILLING:

In the bowl of a stand mixer fitted with the whisk attachment (or in a large bowl with a handheld mixer) on medium speed, whip the eggs, lavender sugar, lemon juice, lime juice, and lemon zest for 2 to 3 minutes, until foamy. Add the flour and dried lavender and mix until just combined.

Pour the filling over the warm crust. Return to the oven and bake for another 30 minutes, until just set. Let cool completely.

TO MAKE THE TOPPING:

Dust with the powdered sugar. Sprinkle with the dried lavender. Cut into 18 bars.

MY CABBAGE SCONES!

PREP TIME: 20 minutes · COOK TIME: 30 minutes · YIELD: 10 scones

Everyone's favorite cabbage merchant almost didn't make it into Ba Sing Se, because the passport attendant knew that one cabbage slug could've destroyed the city's entire ecosystem. When he finally gained entry, he probably wished he hadn't. His bad-luck streak continued when the animals that Aang freed from Ba Sing Se Zoo devoured his wares. But who can blame them? These savory cabbage scones would have anyone hopping like a hungry rabaroo!

CABBAGE FILLING

4 slices bacon

1½ cups grated cabbage

1 tablespoon brown sugar

½ teaspoon salt

¼ teaspoon black pepper

DOUGH

2 cups all-purpose flour, plus more for dusting

1 tablespoon granulated sugar

1 tablespoon baking powder

1 teaspoon garlic powder

½ teaspoon onion powder

½ teaspoon kosher salt

¼ teaspoon black pepper

½ cup (1 stick) cold unsalted butter, cubed

⅔ cup buttermilk

1 large egg

½ cup feta cheese

2 green onions, diced

2 tablespoons heavy cream, for brushing

SPECIAL EQUIPMENT

Pastry cutter

2¾ inch biscuit cutter

Wire rack

TO MAKE THE CABBAGE FILLING:

In a large skillet over medium-high heat, cook the bacon for 4 to 6 minutes, until crispy. Remove from the pan, leaving the oil. Let cool slightly, then crumble. Set aside.

To the same skillet with the bacon grease, add the grated cabbage and cook over medium heat for 2 to 3 minutes to soften. Add the brown sugar, salt, and pepper. Cook for 3 to 4 minutes, until lightly caramelized and browned. Remove from the heat. Set aside.

Preheat the oven to 400°F. Line 2 baking sheets with parchment paper.

TO MAKE THE DOUGH:

In a large bowl, whisk together the flour, granulated sugar, baking powder, garlic powder, onion powder, salt, and pepper. Using a pastry cutter, work in the cold butter until crumbly. Stir in the buttermilk and egg until just combined. Fold in the crumbled bacon, cabbage mixture, feta cheese, and green onions.

On a lightly floured surface, roll out the dough to 1 inch thick. Use a biscuit cutter to cut into 10 rounds, rerolling the dough as needed. Place on the prepped baking sheets. Brush the scones with heavy cream.

Bake for 20 minutes, until golden brown. Let cool on a wire rack.

CRAB PUFFS

PREP TIME: 20 minutes · COOK TIME: 15 minutes · YIELD: 48 puffs

It wasn't easy to get an audience with the monarch of the Earth Kingdom, even for the Avatar. When King Kuei threw a lavish party for his pet bear, Bosco, Team Avatar snuck inside to get a little face time with His Royal Highness. While their plan didn't work out quite as they'd hoped, at least they got some delicious crab puffs. They prove that you can always find fun flavors in life, even when things go awry!

PASTRY

1 sheet (8.65 ounces) of frozen puff pastry, thawed

EGG WASH

1 egg

1 tablespoon water

FILLING

4 ounces cream cheese, softened

¼ cup Greek yogurt

2 tablespoons furikake seasoning

1 teaspoon Dijon mustard

1 teaspoon lemon juice

1 teaspoon Worcestershire sauce

¼ teaspoon kosher salt

¼ teaspoon ground black pepper

8 ounces crabmeat, drained and flaked

GARNISH

½ cup sweet chili sauce

1 tablespoon chopped fresh parsley

SPECIAL EQUIPMENT

Two 24-count mini muffin pans

Pastry brush

Preheat the oven to 400°F. Coat two 24-count mini muffin pans with nonstick spray.

TO MAKE THE PASTRY:
Roll out the pastry sheet to 15 inches by 15 inches and cut it into squares (approximately 1¼ inch by 1¼ inch), totaling 48 pieces. Press the pieces into the prepped pans.

TO MAKE THE EGG WASH:
In a small bowl, whisk together the egg and water. Brush the egg wash on the pastry pieces. Set aside.

TO MAKE THE FILLING:
In a large bowl, combine the cream cheese, Greek yogurt, furikake, Dijon mustard, lemon juice, Worcestershire sauce, salt, and pepper. Gently fold in the crabmeat. Add a spoonful of the crab mixture to the center of each puff pastry.

Bake for 15 minutes, until golden brown. Let cool slightly.

TO GARNISH:
Dollop a teaspoon of the sweet chili sauce onto each crab puff. Sprinkle with the parsley.

BAKED PLUMS

V · PREP TIME: 30 minutes, plus 1 hour chilling · COOK TIME: 45 minutes · YIELD: 8 servings

Sokka may be the last person you'd expect to compete in a haiku poetry duel. But he managed to hold his own when he stumbled across the Five-Seven-Five Society. These baked plums would make a lovely snack at any artistic event. It's just like Madame Macmu-Ling said: "There's nuts and there's fruits / in the fall, the clean plum drops, / always to be squashed." (Whatever that means.)

PÂTE BRISÉE

1⅔ cups all-purpose flour, plus more for dusting

¼ teaspoon kosher salt

¾ cup (1½ sticks) cold unsalted butter, cubed

6 tablespoons ice water

FILLING

8 plums, pitted and sliced (2½ cups)

¼ cup packed light brown sugar

1 tablespoon cornstarch

½ teaspoon ground cinnamon

¼ teaspoon ground cloves

2 teaspoons lemon juice

1 teaspoon vanilla extract

1 tablespoon honey

EGG WASH

1 large egg

1 tablespoon water

2 teaspoons coarse sanding sugar

SPECIAL EQUIPMENT

Pastry cutter

Pastry brush

Wire rack

TO MAKE THE PÂTE BRISÉE:

In a large bowl, combine the flour and salt. Use a pastry cutter to cut in the butter until crumbly. Add the water, 1 tablespoon at a time, until the dough comes together. Pat into a disk and wrap in plastic wrap. Chill in the refrigerator for 1 hour.

TO MAKE THE FILLING:

In a large bowl, combine the sliced plums, brown sugar, cornstarch, cinnamon, cloves, lemon juice, and vanilla. Set aside.

Preheat the oven to 375°F. Line a baking sheet with parchment paper.

Remove the dough from the refrigerator. On a lightly floured surface, roll out the dough to a 13-inch diameter. Arrange the plums in a pattern on the dough circle, leaving a 2-inch border around the edge. Drizzle with any remaining juice from the plums. Drizzle with the honey. Fold the edges of the dough up and over the sides of the plums, leaving the center of the galette open.

TO MAKE THE EGG WASH:

In a small bowl, whisk together the egg and water. Brush the egg wash on the dough. Sprinkle with the coarse sugar.

Bake for 45 minutes, until the crust is golden brown. Let cool on a wire rack.

SIZZLE CRISPY TREATS

V · PREP TIME: 15 minutes · COOK TIME: 20 minutes · YIELD: 24 servings

A bag of meaty sizzle-crisps may have been a crowd-favorite snack at a Fire Nation circus, but for attendees like Aang—a devoted vegetarian—this menu item didn't offer the same draw as watching the animals. This dessert variation of the sizzle-crisp is made from spiced puffed rice. It's not as hot as flying through a flaming hoop on a "Wind Buffalo," but it still keeps a bit of that signature sizzle-crisp heat alongside the sweet.

½ cup (1 stick) unsalted butter, sliced

10 ounces vegan marshmallows

2 tablespoons nori komi furikake seasoning, divided

1 teaspoon togarashi seasoning

4 cups rice cereal

2 cups cornflakes

¾ cup chili rice crackers

Preheat the oven to 350°F. Line a baking sheet with parchment paper and coat with nonstick spray.

Evenly space uniform slices of the butter across the prepared baking sheet. Spread the marshmallows out in an even layer. Bake for 15 minutes, until the marshmallows are lightly browned and have puffed up. Remove from the oven. Sprinkle the baked marshmallows with 1 tablespoon of the furikake and all of the togarashi.

Pour the rice cereal and cornflakes onto the baked marshmallows, tossing gently to coat. Fold in the chili rice crackers.

Press the cereal mix into the marshmallow pan and sprinkle on the remaining 1 tablespoon of furikake. Let cool. Cut into squares.

DRAGON OF THE WEST TEA CAKE

V · PREP TIME: 30 minutes · COOK TIME: 1 hour 10 minutes · YIELD: 8 servings

Long before Iroh opened the finest tea shop in Ba Sing Se, the Jasmine Dragon, he was a respected Fire Nation general. He supposedly earned the nickname "The Dragon of the West" due to his impressive ability to spew fire from his mouth. This spiced tea cake, named in his honor, may only make your mouth tingle a bit, but it's still worthy of being served in the most celebrated tea shops in any nation.

TEA CAKE

2 cups all-purpose flour

1 cup packed light brown sugar

1 cup granulated sugar

1½ teaspoons baking powder

2 teaspoons ground cinnamon

1 teaspoon ground ginger

½ teaspoon ground allspice

½ teaspoon ground nutmeg

¼ teaspoon ground cayenne

¼ teaspoon ground cloves

½ teaspoon kosher salt

¾ cup vegetable oil

½ cup sour cream

4 large eggs

1 teaspoon vanilla extract

2½ cups grated carrots, plus more for garnish

¾ cup chopped pecans, plus more for garnish

FROSTING

8 ounces cream cheese, softened

4 tablespoons unsalted butter, softened

2 cups powdered sugar

½ teaspoon vanilla extract

¼ teaspoon kosher salt

⅓ cup heavy whipping cream

1 tablespoon hot honey

SPECIAL EQUIPMENT

9-by-5-inch loaf pan

Stand mixer or handheld mixer

Piping bag and star tip

Preheat the oven to 350°F. Coat a 9-by-5-inch loaf pan with nonstick spray.

TO MAKE THE TEA CAKE:

In a large bowl, whisk together the flour, brown sugar, granulated sugar, baking powder, cinnamon, ginger, allspice, nutmeg, cayenne, cloves, and salt. Make a well in the center of the dry ingredients and add the oil, sour cream, eggs, and vanilla. Stir until just combined. Fold in the carrots and pecans. Spoon the batter into the prepped pan.

Bake for 60 to 70 minutes, until a toothpick inserted into the center of the cake comes out clean. Let cool completely.

TO MAKE THE FROSTING:

In the bowl of a stand mixer fitted with the paddle attachment (or in a large bowl with a handheld mixer) on medium speed, beat the cream cheese, butter, powdered sugar, vanilla, and salt. Slowly add the heavy whipping cream and beat for 2 minutes, until light and fluffy.

Transfer the frosting to a piping bag fitted with a star tip. Pipe small star-shaped dollops of frosting on top of the cake. Add pecans and grated carrots, then drizzle with hot honey and serve.

BOOK THREE

RECIPES FROM THE THIRD CHAPTER IN AVATAR AANG'S JOURNEY

By now, you've come a long way in your journey, just like Aang and his friends. At the start of Book Three, Aang awoke aboard a Fire Nation ship to a world that believed him to be gone. It's a discovery similar to the one he made when he first emerged from an iceberg in the South Pole. But this time, he had a team of friends waiting for him, as well as countless lessons he could draw on from their adventures together. It wasn't just Aang facing the effects of Sozin's Comet or Azula's coronation, it was all of Team Avatar.

As you reach for recipes in the final section of the book, trust that you have all the skills and knowledge you need right at your fingertips. Trust that your past experiences in the kitchen are there to keep you company as you try your hand at Sozin's Comet Macarons or Coronation Cherry Piece. And if your gut is telling you to take a new approach with a recipe, follow it. After all, in baking, just like in bending, there's room to take ancient techniques in bold new directions. We can give you the recipes, but it's up to you to tap into your own inventiveness and determination to bring them to life and chart your own destiny!

CRESCENT ISLAND CRESCENTS

V · PREP TIME: 30 minutes, plus 1 hour chilling time · COOK TIME: 20 minutes
YIELD: 32 crescents

Long ago, Crescent Island was the home of Roku, the Avatar who preceded Aang. After Roku's death, Fire Sages remained to guard the Fire Temple on the island, until it was eventually destroyed in a volcanic eruption. These chocolate crescents, filled with a raspberry jam that flows like lava, are probably the closest anyone should get to this flaming isle.

2 cups all-purpose flour, plus more for dusting

½ cup granulated sugar

¼ cup unsweetened cocoa powder

1 teaspoon active dry yeast

½ cup (1 stick) unsalted butter, cubed

½ cup sour cream

2 egg yolks

½ teaspoon almond extract

1 cup raspberry jam

¼ cup powdered sugar, for dusting

SPECIAL EQUIPMENT

Stand mixer or handheld mixer

Pizza cutter

Wire rack

In the bowl of a stand mixer fitted with the paddle attachment (or in a large bowl with a handheld mixer) on medium speed, combine the flour, granulated sugar, cocoa powder, and yeast. Add the butter and beat until crumbly. Beat in the sour cream, egg yolks, and almond extract. Beat for 3 to 4 minutes, until smooth. Divide the dough in half and shape into disks. Wrap both in plastic wrap and refrigerate for 1 hour.

Preheat the oven to 350°F. Line 2 baking sheets with parchment paper.

On a floured surface, roll out one disk of dough to a 12-inch circle. Spread half the jam over the entire surface of the dough. Use a pizza cutter to cut the dough into 16 triangles. Starting at the wide end, roll up each triangle into a crescent shape and place on the prepared baking sheets. Repeat with the remaining dough and jam.

Bake for 20 minutes, until lightly browned. Let cool on a wire rack. Dust with powdered sugar just before serving.

FLAMEY-Os

PREP TIME: 35 minutes · COOK TIME: 30 minutes · YIELD: 12 donuts

To traverse the Fire Nation safely, Team Avatar had to find ways to blend in. A change of clothes helped, but Aang went a step further—maybe too far!—and embraced Fire Nation slang (or at least what he remembered of it from a hundred years before . . .). A lot may have changed in a century, but apparently dancing the Camelephant Strut is timeless and eventually helped Aang win over the local kids. You can, too, with these baked donuts that'll have every "hotman" shouting "Flamey-O!" at *your* next dance party.

BACON CRUMBLE

3 slices bacon

2 tablespoons light brown sugar

¼ teaspoon cayenne pepper

DONUTS

1 cup all-purpose flour

⅔ cup granulated sugar

1 teaspoon baking powder

½ teaspoon ground cinnamon

¼ teaspoon nutmeg

¼ teaspoon kosher salt

1 large egg

⅔ cup horchata

½ teaspoon vanilla extract

GLAZE

1 cup powdered sugar

½ teaspoon ground cinnamon

2 tablespoons horchata

1 tablespoon unsalted butter, melted

TOPPING

⅓ cup diced fresh mango

1 teaspoon Tajín seasoning

SPECIAL EQUIPMENT

Wire rack

Two 6-count donut pans

TO MAKE THE BACON CRUMBLE:

Preheat the oven to 375°F. Line a baking sheet with foil, then place a wire rack on top and coat with nonstick spray.

Place the bacon on the prepared wire rack. Sprinkle with the brown sugar and cayenne. Bake for 17 to 20 minutes, until browned. Let cool for 2 to 3 minutes, then crumble. Set aside.

TO MAKE THE DONUTS:

Preheat the oven to 350°F. Coat 2 donut pans with nonstick spray. Set aside.

In a large bowl, whisk together the flour, granulated sugar, baking powder, cinnamon, nutmeg, and salt. Make a well in the center of the dry ingredients and add the egg, horchata, and vanilla. Stir until just combined. Spoon the batter into the prepared pans.

Bake for 12 minutes, until golden brown. Let cool on a wire rack.

TO MAKE THE GLAZE:

In a small bowl, combine the powdered sugar, cinnamon, and horchata. Stir in the melted butter. Drizzle the glaze over the donuts.

TO MAKE THE TOPPING:

Top the freshly glazed donuts with the crumbled bacon and mango and sprinkle with the Tajín.

PAINTED LADY FISH PIE

PREP TIME: 1 hour 45 minutes · COOK TIME: 1 hour 30 minutes · YIELD: 6 servings

The fishing village of Jang Hui sat in the middle of a river polluted by a Fire Nation factory. In order to help the struggling townspeople, Katara dressed up as the legendary river spirit, the Painted Lady, and delivered fresh fish and medicine. This fish *en croûte* incorporates the Painted Lady's signature red-striped face paint for a recipe that's off the hook! (Get it . . . ? Like a fishing hook . . . ?)

SALMON

1 tablespoon olive oil

1 tablespoon unsalted butter

One 1½-pound salmon fillet, 1 inch thick

½ teaspoon kosher salt

¼ teaspoon black pepper

FILLING

2 tablespoons olive oil

1 shallot, minced

1 clove garlic, minced

6 ounces mushrooms, minced

1 cup baby spinach

¼ cup crème fraîche

1 tablespoon minced fresh dill

2 teaspoons lemon zest

½ teaspoon kosher salt

¼ teaspoon black pepper

PIE

One 17.3-ounce package frozen puff pastry, thawed

2 tablespoons red gel food coloring, for decorating

EGG WASH

1 large egg

1 tablespoon water

SPECIAL EQUIPMENT

Pastry brush

TO MAKE THE SALMON:

In a large skillet over medium heat, heat the olive oil and butter until the butter has melted. Add the salmon, skin side up. Season with half the salt and pepper. Cook for 4 to 5 minutes. Flip over, season with the remaining salt and pepper, and cook for 5 minutes more, until it's firm and flakes easily when tested with a fork. Transfer to a plate and let cool. Flake the entire salmon fillet with a fork. Set aside.

TO MAKE THE FILLING:

Wipe out the skillet with a paper towel. Over medium-high heat, heat the olive oil. Add the shallot and garlic and cook for 2 to 3 minutes, until softened. Add the mushrooms and cook for 6 to 8 minutes, until softened. Add the spinach and cook for 2 to 3 minutes, until wilted. Turn off the heat. Stir in the crème fraîche, dill, lemon zest, salt, and pepper. Let cool. Stir in the flaked salmon. Set aside.

TO MAKE THE PIE:

On a lightly floured surface, roll out one sheet of puff pastry. Cut into a 9-inch circle. Transfer to a parchment-lined baking sheet. Add the salmon mixture in the center of the puff pastry, spreading it into an 8-inch circle.

Roll out the second piece of puff pastry. Cut into a 9.75-inch circle. Lay over the salmon mixture, pressing the edges of the top and bottom pastry together to seal.

Use a pastry brush and the red gel food coloring to paint the Painted Lady's face markings on top of the pastry. Refrigerate for 1 hour.

Preheat the oven to 400°F.

TO MAKE THE EGG WASH:

In a small bowl, whisk together the egg and water. Brush the pastry with the egg wash. Cut a slit in the center to vent.

Bake for 25 to 30 minutes, until golden brown. Transfer to a serving platter.

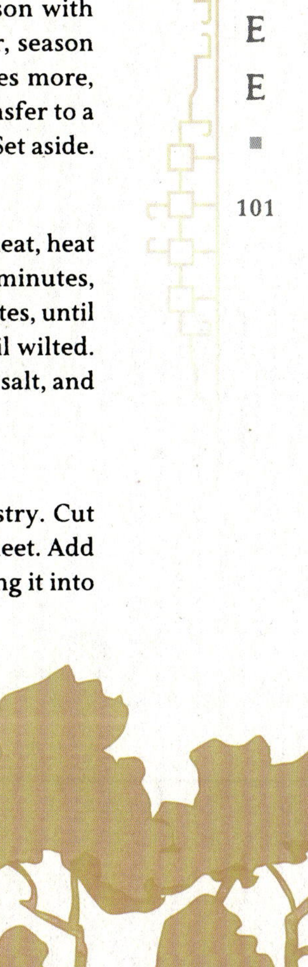

FILLED FISH CAKES

V · PREP TIME: 10 minutes · COOK TIME: 10 minutes · YIELD: 12 fish cakes

Here's another way to pay tribute to the Jang Hui River's spirit, the Painted Lady. For those who'd prefer a vegetarian alternative to Painted Lady Fish Pie (page 101), consider these tiny sweet cakes filled with red bean paste and baked in a fish-shaped pan. No actual fish—or spirit magic—necessary! Bake up some of these and you're sure to be everybody's secret hero!

½ cup all-purpose flour
½ cup mochiko flour
2 tablespoons brown sugar
1 teaspoon baking powder
¼ teaspoon kosher salt
⅔ cup whole milk
1 large egg, lightly beaten
½ teaspoon vanilla extract
¼ cup red bean paste

SPECIAL EQUIPMENT
Fish molds or baking pan with fish-shaped wells

Wire rack

Preheat the oven to 350°F. Coat a baking pan with fish-shaped wells with nonstick spray

In a large bowl, whisk together the flour, mochiko, brown sugar, baking powder, and salt. Make a well in the center of the dry ingredients and add the milk, egg, and vanilla and stir until just combined.

Fill each of the fish-shaped wells with 1 tablespoon of the batter. Add 1 teaspoon of the red bean paste to each, then spoon over another 1 tablespoon of batter to cover the red bean paste in each well.

Bake for 10 minutes, until golden brown. Let cool on a wire rack.

SPACE EARTH SHORTBREAD

V · PREP TIME: 30 minutes, plus 1 hour chilling time · COOK TIME: 15 minutes
YIELD: 24 cookies

When a meteorite crashed to Earth, Sokka used its mysterious metal to forge the blade of his new sword. He saved Toph a small chunk, which she eagerly metalbent into the shape of a star. These star-shaped shortbread cookies don't contain any "space earth" (though, to be fair, if it's from space, is it really earth anyway?), but they do have a flavor that's out of this world!

1¾ cups all-purpose flour, plus more for dusting

⅓ cup unsweetened cocoa powder

2 tablespoons ground black sesame seeds

¼ teaspoon kosher salt

1 cup (2 sticks) unsalted butter

1 cup powdered sugar

SPECIAL EQUIPMENT

Stand mixer or handheld mixer

Star-shaped cookie cutter (optional)

Preheat the oven to 350°F. Line 2 baking sheets with parchment paper.

In a large bowl, whisk together the flour, cocoa powder, ground black sesame seeds, and salt.

In the bowl of a stand mixer fitted with the paddle attachment (or in a large bowl with a handheld mixer) on medium speed, cream the butter and powdered sugar until fluffy. Add the dry ingredients and beat until just combined. Wrap the dough in plastic wrap and refrigerate for 1 hour.

On a lightly floured surface, roll out the dough to ½ inch thick. Use a star-shaped cookie cutter, or cut into star shapes by hand, to cut out 24 cookies, rerolling the scraps as needed. Place on the prepared baking sheets.

Bake for 12 to 15 minutes, until the cookies are just set. Let cool on the baking sheets.

EMBER ISLAND CONCHAS

V · PREP TIME: 2 hours 30 minutes · COOK TIME: 20 minutes · YIELD: 12 buns

It's said that a trip to Ember Island smooths a person's jagged edges and reveals one's true self. One thing it revealed to Zuko and friends was how questionable some people's decorating choices were. The pink seashell bedspread in Li and Lo's summer home may have looked like the beach threw up all over it, but these seashell-inspired *conchas* (Mexican sweet breads) are in far better taste!

TOPPING

½ cup (1 stick) unsalted butter, softened

⅔ cup sugar

1 cup all-purpose flour

3 tablespoons ground freeze-dried strawberries

1 teaspoon almond extract

2 drops pink gel food coloring

BREAD

1 envelope (2¼ teaspoons) active dry yeast

¾ cup whole milk, heated to 110°F

½ cup (1 stick) unsalted butter, softened

⅓ cup sugar

½ teaspoon kosher salt

2 large eggs

1 teaspoon vanilla extract

3½ cups bread flour, plus more for dusting

2 tablespoons olive oil, for greasing

SPECIAL EQUIPMENT

Stand mixer

Instant-read thermometer

Wire rack

TO MAKE THE TOPPING:

In the bowl of a stand mixer fitted with the paddle attachment (or in a large bowl with a handheld mixer) on medium speed, cream the butter and sugar until combined. Slowly add the flour and beat until just combined. Add the ground strawberries, almond extract, and pink gel food coloring and beat until just combined. Divide into 12 equal balls. Transfer to a parchment-lined baking sheet. Refrigerate until ready to use.

TO MAKE THE BREAD:

In the bowl of a stand mixer fitted with a dough hook, sprinkle the yeast over the warm milk and let sit for 10 minutes, until foamy.

With the mixer on medium speed, add the butter, sugar, salt, eggs, and vanilla. Slowly add the 3½ cups bread flour and mix until combined. Raise the mixer speed to medium-high and knead for 5 to 8 minutes, until smooth and elastic.

Place the dough in a large bowl greased with olive oil, turning to coat. Cover with plastic wrap and let rise for 1½ hours, until doubled in size.

Punch down the dough and turn out onto a floured surface. Divide into 12 equal pieces and roll into balls. These will serve as the buns. Cover with a tea towel while you return to the topping.

Remove the topping from the refrigerator. Place one strawberry topping ball between 2 sheets of parchment paper. Roll out into a 3-inch circle. Gently place it on top of a dough bun. Use a paring knife to score a traditional concha shell design. Repeat with the remaining strawberry topping balls and dough buns. Place on a parchment-lined baking sheet. Cover with a tea towel. Let rise for 1 hour.

Preheat the oven to 350°F.

Bake the buns for 18 to 20 minutes, until an instant-read thermometer registers 190°F. Let cool on a wire rack and serve while still warm.

KOMODO SAUSAGES

PREP TIME: 2 hours 20 minutes · COOK TIME: 15 minutes · YIELD: 8 servings

Two master Waterbenders, under a full moon, ought to be able to handle anything . . . at least according to Hama, the mysterious innkeeper who offered to train Katara. For Katara, *anything* included securing some free komodo sausages from Mr. Yao's market stand. For Hama, it went much further, extending to the forbidden act of bloodbending. With this recipe, you can just make your own tiny sausages without a full moon or a dangerous mentor . . .

DOUGH

1 teaspoon active dry yeast

¾ cup whole milk, heated to 110°F

2 cups all-purpose flour

2 teaspoons sugar

¼ teaspoon kosher salt

1 tablespoon olive oil, for greasing

FILLING

8 lap cheong sausages, plastic removed

EGG WASH

1 large egg

1 tablespoon water

GLAZE

1 tablespoon sugar

1 tablespoon warm water

SPECIAL EQUIPMENT

Stand mixer

Pastry brush

Wire rack

TO MAKE THE DOUGH:

In the bowl of a stand mixer fitted with a dough hook, sprinkle the yeast over the warm milk. Let sit for 10 minutes, until foamy.

With the mixer on medium speed, add the flour, sugar, and salt and mix until just combined. Raise the mixer speed to medium-high and knead for 5 minutes, until elastic.

Shape into a ball, then place into a bowl greased with olive oil, turning to coat. Cover the bowl with plastic wrap and let rise for 1 hour, until doubled in size.

Punch down the dough, turn out onto a floured surface, and knead for 2 minutes, until smooth. Divide into 8 equal pieces. Roll each piece into a 16-inch-long rope.

TO MAKE THE FILLING:

Wrap a dough rope around one lap cheong, starting at the bottom and ending at the top. Place on a baking sheet lined with parchment paper. Repeat with the remaining dough and sausages.
Cover with a tea towel and let rise for 1 hour.

Preheat the oven to 350°F.

TO MAKE THE EGG WASH:

In a small bowl, whisk together the egg and water. Brush onto the buns.

Bake for 12 to 15 minutes, until golden brown.

TO MAKE THE GLAZE:

In a separate small bowl, whisk together the sugar and water. Immediately brush onto the warm buns. Let cool on a wire rack.

ASH BANANA BREAD

V · PREP TIME: 25 minutes · COOK TIME: 1 hour · YIELD: 8 servings

Ash bananas aren't easy to find. Merchants have to send someone to Hing Wa Island to get them and then hope that their courier doesn't get lost in the woods during a full moon, falling victim to evil spirits or a dark puppet master. It's a lot. For those understandably reluctant to wait a week for ash bananas, we recommend using regular bananas to make this delicious bread.

BREAD

1⅔ cups all-purpose flour

1 cup granulated sugar

1 teaspoon baking soda

¼ teaspoon kosher salt

2 ripe medium bananas, mashed

½ cup (1 stick) unsalted butter, melted

½ cup sour cream

2 large eggs, lightly beaten

1 teaspoon vanilla extract

2 tablespoons black sesame paste

GLAZE

2 ounces cream cheese, softened

1 tablespoon unsalted butter, softened

½ cup powdered sugar

1 tablespoon ground black sesame seeds

1 tablespoon black sesame paste

2 tablespoons whole milk

½ teaspoon whole black sesame seeds, for decorating

SPECIAL EQUIPMENT

9-by-5-inch loaf pan

Instant-read thermometer

Handheld mixer

Preheat the oven to 350°F. Line a 9-by-5-inch loaf pan with parchment paper and coat with nonstick spray.

TO MAKE THE BREAD:

In a large bowl, whisk together the flour, granulated sugar, baking soda, and salt. Make a well in the center of the dry ingredients and add the bananas, butter, sour cream, eggs, and vanilla. Stir until just combined. Set aside ½ cup of the batter. To the remaining batter, stir in the black sesame paste, then spoon the black sesame batter into the prepped loaf pan. Dollop the reserved plain batter along the top of the black sesame batter. Use a toothpick to swirl the two batters together on top.

Bake for 60 minutes, or until an instant-read thermometer inserted into the center of the bread reads 200°F. Let cool.

TO MAKE THE GLAZE:

In a medium bowl, using a handheld mixer, beat the cream cheese and butter until smooth. Add the powdered sugar, ground black sesame seeds, and black sesame paste and beat until combined. Add the milk and beat until smooth and pourable.

Pour the glaze over the cooled cake. Sprinkle with the black sesame seeds.

PEANUT SAUCE BOMBS

V · PREP TIME: 40 minutes · COOK TIME: 10 minutes · YIELD: 24 servings

Team Avatar called in a number of old friends to help invade the Fire Nation on the Day of Black Sun. The Mechanist from the Northern Air Temple brought a few new inventions along for the battle, including a prototype peanut-sauce bomb. The incendiary capabilities of peanut sauce didn't live up to expectations, but these cookies will! And they prove that peanuts can be delicious without being destructive!

½ cup (1 stick) unsalted butter, softened

½ cup creamy peanut butter

½ cup granulated sugar, plus more for rolling

½ cup packed light brown sugar

2 large eggs

1 teaspoon vanilla extract

1½ cups all-purpose flour

½ cup unsweetened cocoa powder

½ teaspoon baking soda

¼ teaspoon kosher salt

24 miniature peanut butter cups, unwrapped

SPECIAL EQUIPMENT

Stand mixer or handheld mixer

Preheat the oven to 350°F. Line a baking sheet with parchment paper.

In the bowl of a stand mixer fitted with the paddle attachment (or in a large bowl with a handheld mixer) on medium speed, cream the butter, peanut butter, granulated sugar, and brown sugar until fluffy. Add the eggs and vanilla and beat until combined.

In a medium bowl, whisk together the flour, cocoa powder, baking soda, and salt. Add to the butter mixture and beat until just combined. Refrigerate the dough for 20 minutes.

Scoop out 2 tablespoons of dough, shape into a ball, and flatten into a circle. Place a peanut butter cup in the center. Pull up the edges of the dough around the peanut butter cup to seal. Roll in granulated sugar and place on the prepared baking sheet. Repeat with the remaining dough and peanut butter cups.

Bake the cookies for 10 minutes, until just set. Let the cookies cool on the baking sheet.

GLIDER SNACKS

V · PREP TIME: 15 minutes · COOK TIME: 15 minutes · YIELD: 36 cookies

After Aang burned his original glider staff on Crescent Island, the Mechanist and his son, Teo, crafted the Avatar a new glider with an unexpected upgrade—a hidden snack compartment! With just a turn of a handle, tiny treats went tumbling into Aang's mouth. It sure came in handy to cure the mid-flight munchies! These bite-size chocolate chip cookies are a perfect fit anywhere you store your snacks.

1¼ cups all-purpose flour

½ teaspoon baking powder

⅛ teaspoon kosher salt

½ cup (1 stick) unsalted butter, softened

½ cup powdered sugar, plus more for dusting

1 large egg

1 teaspoon vanilla extract

½ cup mini chocolate chips

¼ cup chopped pecans

SPECIAL EQUIPMENT

Stand mixer or handheld mixer

Wire rack

Preheat the oven to 350°F. Line 2 baking sheets with parchment paper.

In a large bowl, whisk together the flour, baking powder, and salt.

In the bowl of a stand mixer fitted with the paddle attachment (or in a large bowl with a handheld mixer) on medium speed, cream the butter and powdered sugar until light and fluffy. Add the egg and vanilla and beat until combined. Gradually add the flour mixture and beat until just combined. Fold in the mini chocolate chips and chopped pecans.

Scoop out and form teaspoon-size balls of dough. Transfer to the prepared baking sheet, leaving 1 inch of space between the balls.

Bake for 13 to 15 minutes, until lightly browned. Let cool on a wire rack. Dust with powdered sugar just before serving.

WHITE JADE TEA PUFFS

V · PREP TIME: 3 hours 45 minutes, plus 24 hours steeping · COOK TIME: 15 minutes
YIELD: 10 buns

While Iroh was held captive at the Capital City Prison, a kind guard named Ming snuck in some rare teas to make his days more bearable. When Ming brought him white jade tea, Iroh didn't tell her how poisonous it was. Instead, he rewarded her well-meaning gesture by warning her she might want to go home and rest during the Day of Black Sun. Inspired by those little acts of kindness on both sides, these sweet buns hold a refreshing tea and cream filling, making them a poison-free way to brighten somebody's day.

FILLING

1 cup heavy whipping cream

2 black tea bags

8 ounces mascarpone cheese

1 cup powdered sugar

½ teaspoon vanilla extract

ROUX

1 black tea bag

½ cup warm water

3 tablespoons bread flour

SPECIAL EQUIPMENT

Stand mixer or handheld mixer

TO MAKE THE FILLING:

Pour the heavy cream into a mason jar and add the tea bags. Cover and refrigerate overnight until ready to use. After steeping, remove and discard the tea bags.

In the bowl of a stand mixer fitted with the whisk attachment (or in a large bowl with a handheld mixer) on medium-high speed, whip the infused heavy cream for 2 to 3 minutes, until soft peaks form. Set aside.

In a medium bowl, combine the mascarpone cheese, powdered sugar, and vanilla and stir until smooth. Fold the mascarpone mixture into the whipped cream until combined. Whip again for 1 minute, until fluffy and fully incorporated. Refrigerate until ready to use.

TO MAKE THE ROUX:

Steep the tea bag in the warm water for 5 minutes. Discard the tea bag. In a saucepan over medium heat, whisk together the tea and bread flour for 1 minute, until thickened. Turn off the heat. Transfer the roux to a bowl. Set aside to cool.

BOOK THREE ■ 114

DOUGH

1 envelope (2¼ teaspoons) active dry yeast

¾ cup whole milk, heated to 110°F

4 tablespoons unsalted butter, melted

¼ cup sweetened condensed milk

½ teaspoon kosher salt

1 large egg, lightly beaten

Roux (see recipe on page 113)

3½ cups bread flour, plus more for dusting

2 tablespoons olive oil, for greasing

EGG WASH

1 large egg

1 tablespoon water

GLAZE

1 cup fine desiccated coconut

2 tablespoons granulated sugar

2 tablespoons boiling water

SPECIAL EQUIPMENT

Mason jar with lid

Handheld mixer, optional

Stand mixer

Wire rack

Serrated knife

Pastry brush

Piping bag with a star tip

TO MAKE THE DOUGH:

In the bowl of a stand mixer fitted with a dough hook, sprinkle the yeast over the warm milk and let sit for 10 minutes, until foamy. Add the butter, condensed milk, salt, egg, and roux and mix until combined. Slowly add the flour and mix until combined. Knead for 8 to 10 minutes until smooth and elastic.

Place the dough in a large bowl greased with the olive oil, turning the dough to coat. Cover the bowl and let rise for 1 hour, until doubled in size.

Punch down the dough and turn out onto a lightly floured surface. Divide into 10 equal portions and roll into balls. Place on a parchment-lined baking sheet and cover with a tea towel. Let rise for 45 minutes.

On a lightly floured surface, roll out one dough ball into a 6-inch-long oval. Roll up the sides lengthwise, creating a narrow oblong bun. Place the bun, seam side down, back on the parchment-lined baking sheet. Repeat with the remaining dough balls, spacing them 3 inches apart (you might need 2 baking sheets for this). Cover baking sheets with tea towels. Let rise for another 45 minutes.

Preheat the oven to 350°F.

TO MAKE THE EGG WASH:

In a small bowl, whisk together the egg and water. Brush the egg wash on the tops of the buns.

Bake for 12 to 15 minutes, until golden. Let cool on a wire rack.

With a long serrated bread knife, slice the buns down the middle lengthwise, but not all the way through. Let cool slightly.

TO MAKE THE GLAZE:

Spread the coconut on a shallow plate. In a small bowl, stir together the granulated sugar and water. Immediately brush onto the buns, then dip each bun into the coconut. Let cool.

Transfer the filling to a piping bag fitted with a star tip. Pipe the filling in a shell pattern down the cut-open center of each bun. Serve immediately.

HIPPO-COW CAKE

V · PREP TIME: 30 minutes, plus 4 hours chilling time
COOK TIME: 30 minutes · YIELD: 12 servings

The Fire Nation's diet wasn't exactly what Aang was used to at the Air Nomad temples. According to Sokka, everyone there ate meat . . . even the meat! Luckily, carnivorous animals like the hippo cow still produced milk, which meant a vegetarian like Aang had more options than just getting "some lettuce out of the garbage." This milk-soaked tres leches cake is so sweet and decadent that even a nightmare about Fire Lord Ozai on a flying, fire-breathing hippo cow wouldn't scare us off!

CAKE

1½ cups all-purpose flour

2 teaspoons baking powder

½ teaspoon kosher salt

6 large eggs, separated, at room temperature

1¼ cups granulated sugar, divided

1 teaspoon vanilla extract

¼ teaspoon coconut extract

½ teaspoon cream of tartar

MILK SOAK

1 cup whole milk

One 14-ounce can sweetened condensed milk

One 13.5-ounce can coconut milk

WHIPPED CREAM

1½ cups heavy whipping cream

3 tablespoons powdered sugar

¾ cup finely crushed chocolate cookies

SPECIAL EQUIPMENT

Stand mixer or handheld mixer

13-by-9-inch pan

Preheat the oven to 350°F. Line a 13-by-9-inch pan with parchment paper, then lightly coat with nonstick spray.

TO MAKE THE CAKE:

In a medium bowl, whisk together the flour, baking powder, and salt. Set aside.

In the bowl of a stand mixer fitted with the whisk attachment (or in a large bowl with a handheld mixer) on medium speed, whip the egg yolks and half the granulated sugar for 2 to 3 minutes, until light in color. Add the vanilla and coconut extracts. Slowly add the dry mixture and whip until just combined. Set aside.

In a separate bowl of the stand mixer fitted with the whisk attachment (or in a large bowl with a handheld mixer) on medium-high speed, whip the egg whites and cream of tartar until foamy. Slowly add the remaining sugar, whipping until soft peaks form. Gently fold the whipped egg whites into the egg yolk mixture until just combined. Pour the batter into the prepared pan.

Bake for 25 to 30 minutes, until a toothpick inserted into the center of the cake comes out clean. Allow the cake to cool completely.

Use a fork to poke the cake all over.

TO MAKE THE MILK SOAK:

In a large bowl, whisk together the whole milk, sweetened condensed milk, and coconut milk. Gently pour over the cake, allowing the cake to soak up the mixture. Refrigerate the cake for 4 hours.

TO MAKE THE WHIPPED CREAM:

When nearly ready to serve, in a separate bowl of a stand mixer fitted with the whisk attachment (or in a large bowl with a handheld mixer) on medium-high speed, whip the heavy cream and powdered sugar until thickened. Spread over the cake.

Use the crushed cookies to create a hippo-cow pattern on top of the whipped cream.

THE DANCING DRAGON PINEAPPLE BUNS

V · PREP TIME: 2 hours 30 minutes, plus 3 hours chilling time
COOK TIME: 15 minutes · YIELD: 12 buns

The past can be a great teacher, so it's only natural that Aang and Zuko returned to the civilization of the first Firebenders, the Sun Warriors, to learn their ways. There, the pair discovered an ancient firebending form called "the Dancing Dragon technique," illustrated by a ring of statues. When they completed its steps, a giant, glowing gem appeared. These pineapple buns may look like that sunstone, but fortunately they only explode with flavor—not with green, sticky goo!

CUSTARD

¼ cup all-purpose flour

2 tablespoons custard powder

4 large egg yolks

1 cup whole milk

½ cup granulated sugar

2 tablespoons cold unsalted butter, cubed

ROUX

½ cup water

3 tablespoons bread flour

DOUGH

1 envelope (2¼ teaspoons) active dry yeast

¾ cup whole milk, heated to 110°F

4 tablespoons unsalted butter, melted

¼ cup sweetened condensed milk

½ teaspoon kosher salt

1 large egg, lightly beaten

Roux (see recipe above)

3½ cups bread flour, plus more for dusting

2 tablespoons olive oil, for greasing

TO MAKE THE CUSTARD:

In a medium bowl, whisk together the flour, custard powder, and egg yolks until just combined. Set aside.

In a small saucepan over medium heat, whisk together the milk and granulated sugar, cooking for 1 to 2 minutes to a low simmer, until the sugar has dissolved. Decrease the heat to low. Ladle one-third of the hot milk into the egg mixture to temper, whisking until combined. Add the tempered egg mixture to the saucepan.

Whisk constantly until thickened enough to coat the back of a spoon. Remove the pan from the heat. Whisk in the butter. Remove from the heat and pour through a fine-mesh strainer set over a bowl.

Place the bowl into a larger bowl filled with ice, to create an ice bath, and let cool. Once cooled, refrigerate for 3 hours.

Scoop the custard into 12 equal balls. Place on a small parchment-lined baking sheet. Freeze until ready to use.

TO MAKE THE ROUX:

In a saucepan over medium heat, whisk together the water and flour for 1 minute, until thickened. Turn off the heat. Transfer the roux to a bowl. Set aside to cool.

TO MAKE THE DOUGH:

In the bowl of a stand mixer fitted with a dough hook, sprinkle the yeast over the warm milk and let sit for 10 minutes, until foamy.

Add the butter, condensed milk, salt, egg, and roux and mix until combined. Slowly add the flour and mix until combined. Knead for 8 to 10 minutes, until smooth and elastic.

Place the dough in a large bowl greased with olive oil, turning the dough to coat. Cover the bowl with plastic wrap and let rise for 1 hour, until doubled in size.

Line 2 baking sheets with parchment paper. Set aside.

TOPPING

1 cup all-purpose flour

⅔ cup granulated sugar

¼ cup dry buttermilk powder

½ teaspoon baking powder

4 tablespoons unsalted butter, melted

1 large egg yolk

½ teaspoon vanilla extract

2 tablespoons whole milk

EGG WASH

1 large egg yolk

1 tablespoon water

SPECIAL EQUIPMENT

Fine-mesh strainer

Stand mixer

Pastry brush

Wire rack

Punch down the dough and turn out onto a floured surface. Divide into 12 equal portions and roll each into a ball, covering with a tea towel when not in use.

Take one dough ball and flatten into a circle. Place one ball of frozen custard in the center, pulling up the edges of the dough and pinching to close. Place seam side down on the prepared baking sheet. Repeat with the remaining dough and frozen custard balls.

TO MAKE THE TOPPING:

In a large bowl, whisk together the flour, granulated sugar, buttermilk powder, and baking powder. Make a well in the center of the dry ingredients, add the butter, egg yolk, vanilla, and milk, and stir until just combined. Divide into 12 equal balls. Flatten these topping balls into large circles, large enough to cover a dough bun.

Gently place a flattened disk on top of each dough-wrapped custard ball. Use a knife to lightly score the topping in a pineapple pattern. Cover with a tea towel. Let rise for 45 minutes.

Preheat the oven to 350°F.

TO MAKE THE EGG WASH:

In a small bowl, whisk together the egg yolk and water. Brush the egg wash on the top of the buns.

Bake for 12 to 15 minutes, until golden. Let cool on a wire rack.

DRAGON BREATH BUNDT

V · PREP TIME: 20 minutes · COOK TIME: 70 minutes · YIELD: 12 servings

According to the Sun Warriors, dragons were the original Firebenders. Sadly, by the time Avatar Aang returned, they'd been hunted to near extinction. Only two remained, hidden in the cave of the masters, their existence kept secret from the world. Known as Ran and Shaw, the last dragons emerged to reveal their firebending secrets to Aang and Zuko, unleashing beautiful fire in colors the boys could never have imagined. This rainbow Bundt cake tries to capture just a taste of that firebending harmony. Trust us, this one is too good to keep secret!

CAKE

3 cups all-purpose flour

1 teaspoon baking powder

½ teaspoon kosher salt

1 cup (2 sticks) unsalted butter, softened

8 ounces cream cheese, softened

3 cups granulated sugar

6 large eggs

2 teaspoons vanilla extract

4 drops green gel food coloring

4 drops purple gel food coloring

4 drops red gel food coloring

4 drops yellow gel food coloring

ICING

1½ cups powdered sugar

2 tablespoons unsalted butter, melted

½ teaspoon clear vanilla extract

2 tablespoons whole milk

SPECIAL EQUIPMENT

Bundt cake pan

Stand mixer or handheld mixer

Instant-read thermometer

Wire rack

Preheat the oven to 350°F. Grease a Bundt cake pan with nonstick spray.

TO MAKE THE CAKE:

In a large bowl, whisk together the flour, baking powder, and salt. Set aside.

In the bowl of a stand mixer fitted with the paddle attachment (or in a large bowl with a handheld mixer) on medium speed, cream the butter and cream cheese until creamy and smooth. Add the granulated sugar and beat until just combined. Add the eggs, one at a time, beating until combined, then add the vanilla. Decrease the speed to low and gradually add the flour mixture, beating until just combined.

Divide the batter equally among 4 bowls. Add one color of gel food coloring to each bowl, stirring until incorporated.

Drop the batters, alternating colors and ½ cup at a time, into the prepared Bundt pan. Use a butter knife to make figure-eight shapes, swirling the batter in the pan. Tap lightly on the counter to release air bubbles. Place the Bundt pan on a baking sheet.

Bake for 60 to 70 minutes, until the cake is golden and an instant-read thermometer inserted near the center of the cake registers 200°F. Transfer to a wire rack and let cool for 25 minutes.

Gently turn out the cake and let cool completely.

TO MAKE THE ICING:

In a small bowl, whisk together the powdered sugar, melted butter, and clear vanilla. Stir in the milk, 1 tablespoon at a time, until combined. Drizzle the icing over the cake.

TOMATO SOUP CAKES

V · PREP TIME: 20 minutes · COOK TIME: 17 minutes · YIELD: 18 cupcakes

The retired commander of the Southern Raiders, Yon Rha, returned to the Fire Nation to tend to his garden . . . and his overbearing mother. When the tomato-carrots he grew were too hard for her gums, she demanded something soft and juicy instead. These mini tomato soup cakes, topped with cream cheese frosting and an edible flower, are so good, even Yon Rha's mother wouldn't be able to find anything to complain about. Forget your stupid garden and get your grimy heinie into the kitchen to bake a batch!

CUPCAKES

2½ cups cake flour
2 teaspoons baking powder
½ teaspoon baking soda
1½ teaspoons ground cinnamon
½ teaspoon ground allspice
¼ teaspoon ground cloves
¼ teaspoon ground nutmeg
¼ teaspoon kosher salt
½ cup (1 stick) unsalted butter, softened
1 cup granulated sugar
½ cup packed light brown sugar
2 large eggs
One 10¾-ounce can condensed tomato soup
¼ cup whole milk
½ teaspoon vanilla extract

Preheat the oven to 350°F. Prepare a muffin pan with cupcake liners.

TO MAKE THE CUPCAKES:

In a medium bowl, whisk together the cake flour, baking powder, baking soda, cinnamon, allspice, cloves, nutmeg, and salt. Set aside.

In the bowl of a stand mixer fitted with the paddle attachment (or in a large bowl with a handheld mixer) on medium speed, cream the butter, granulated sugar, and brown sugar until fluffy. Add the eggs, one at a time, and beat until combined. Add the tomato soup, milk, and vanilla and beat until combined. Add the dry ingredients and beat until just combined. Spoon the batter into the prepared liners.

Bake for 15 to 17 minutes, or until a toothpick inserted into the cupcakes comes out clean. Let cool on a wire rack.

FROSTING

8 ounces cream cheese

4 tablespoons unsalted butter, softened

1 tablespoon lemon zest

2 cups powdered sugar

¼ teaspoon kosher salt

1 teaspoon vanilla extract

2 tablespoons heavy whipping cream

1½ tablespoons edible flowers, for garnish

SPECIAL EQUIPMENT

Muffin pan

Cupcake liners

Stand mixer or handheld mixer

Wire rack

TO MAKE THE FROSTING:

In the bowl of a stand mixer fitted with the paddle attachment (or in a large bowl with a handheld mixer) on medium speed, add the cream cheese, butter, and lemon zest and beat until combined. Add the powdered sugar, salt, and vanilla and beat until combined. Add the heavy whipping cream and beat for 2 minutes, until light and fluffy. Frost the cooled cupcakes. Add the edible flowers to garnish, then serve.

BLACK SNOW CAKE

V · PREP TIME: 30 minutes · COOK TIME: 45 minutes · YIELD: 10 servings

Members of the Southern Water Tribe were used to the white, pristine snow of the South Pole, so when black snow began to fall, they knew something troubling was on the horizon. You probably wouldn't want to catch the soot from a fleet of Fire Nation raiders on your tongue, but this cookies 'n' cream cake is sure to get your taste buds tingling.

9 egg whites, at room temperature

1 teaspoon cream of tartar

1½ teaspoons vanilla extract

1½ cups sugar

1 cup cake flour

½ cup finely crushed chocolate cookies

½ teaspoon kosher salt

SPECIAL EQUIPMENT

Stand mixer or handheld mixer

Nonstick tube pan

In the bowl of a stand mixer fitted with the whisk attachment (or in a large bowl with a handheld mixer) on medium speed, beat the egg whites until they form soft peaks. Add the cream of tartar and vanilla extract and mix until combined. Slowly add the sugar, whisking until combined.

In a medium bowl, whisk together the flour, crushed cookies, and salt. Gently fold the mixture into the batter.

Pour the batter into an ungreased nonstick tube pan. Place into a cold oven, then set to 325°F. Bake for 1 hour.

Flip the pan upside down and let the cake cool while still in the pan. When cooled completely, run a knife along the edges and remove from the pan.

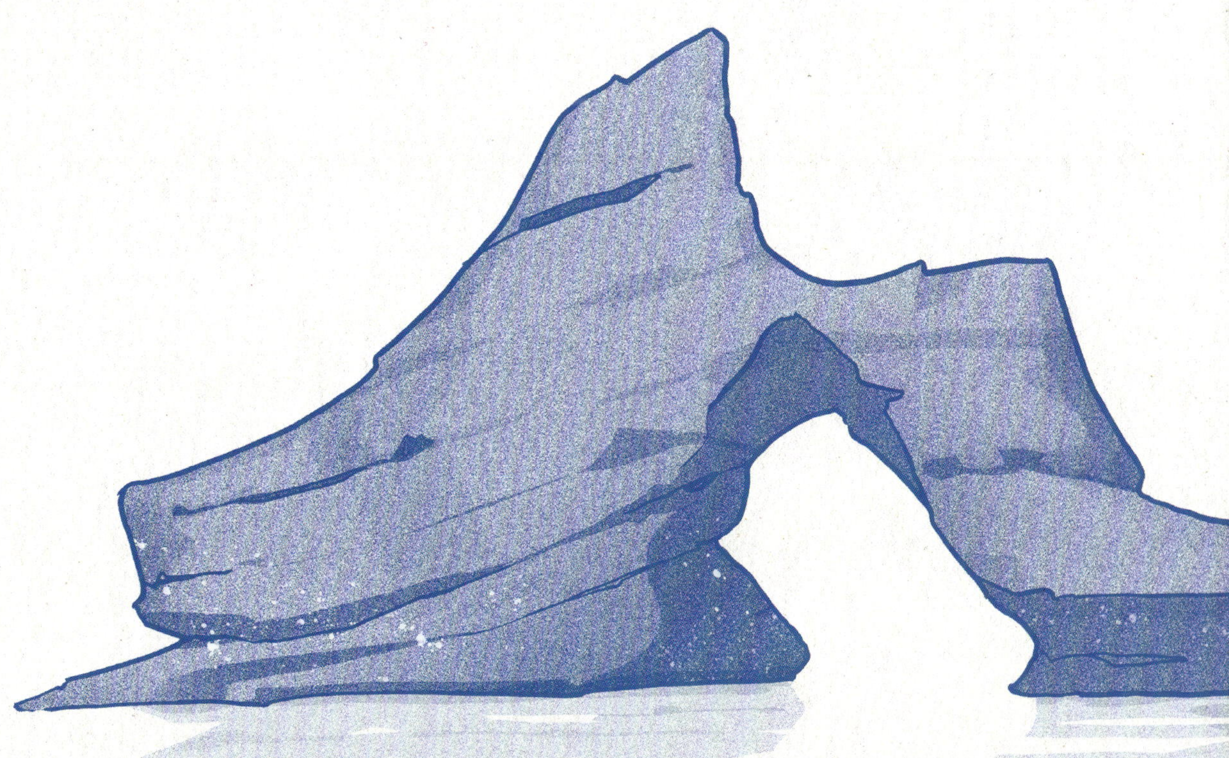

MY CABBAGE CAKES!

V · PREP TIME: 35 minutes · COOK TIME: 20 minutes · YIELD: 12 cupcakes

These cupcakes manage to pay respect to a certain ever-present and surprisingly knowledgeable merchant of cabbage. Complete with a frosting cabbage on top of each one, they are the least we could do after all we watched the poor guy go through!

CUPCAKES

1½ cups all-purpose flour

½ cup packed light brown sugar

½ cup granulated sugar

½ cup unsweetened cocoa powder

1 teaspoon baking soda

½ teaspoon kosher salt

1 cup buttermilk

2 tablespoons strong coffee

6 tablespoons unsalted butter, melted

1 large egg, lightly beaten

½ teaspoon vanilla extract

FROSTING

1 cup (2 sticks) unsalted butter, softened

4 cups powdered sugar

¼ teaspoon kosher salt

1 teaspoon clear vanilla extract

10 tablespoons heavy cream

2 tablespoons plus 1 teaspoon matcha powder

SPECIAL EQUIPMENT

Muffin pan

Cupcake liners

Wire rack

Stand mixer or handheld mixer

Piping bags with flat piping tip and circular piping tip

Preheat the oven to 350°F. Prepare a muffin pan with cupcake liners.

TO MAKE THE CUPCAKES:

In a large bowl, whisk together the flour, brown sugar, granulated sugar, cocoa powder, baking soda, and salt. Make a well in the center of the dry ingredients and add the buttermilk, coffee, melted butter, egg, and vanilla. Stir until just combined. Spoon the batter into the cupcake liners.

Bake for 17 to 20 minutes, until a toothpick inserted into the center of the cupcakes comes out clean. Let cool on a wire rack.

TO MAKE THE FROSTING:

In the bowl of a stand mixer fitted with the paddle attachment (or in a large bowl with a handheld mixer) on medium speed, beat the butter and powdered sugar until fluffy. Add the salt, vanilla, and heavy cream and beat for 1 minute, until fluffy.

Transfer ¾ cup of the frosting to a small bowl. Stir in 1 teaspoon of the matcha powder. Set aside.

To the remaining frosting, stir in the remaining 2 tablespoons of matcha until just combined. Add a dollop of this to the center of each cupcake. Transfer the rest of this darker frosting to a piping bag fitted with a large flat piping tip. Pipe one large leaf shape around the dollop of icing. Continue to create 6 or 7 leaves, overlapping each other around the edges to create a cabbage shape.

Transfer the reserved, lighter frosting to a piping bag fitted with a small circular tip. Use this to add fine lines to give each cabbage leaf details. When the frosting is set, the cupcakes are ready to serve.

SOZIN'S COMET MACARONS

V · PREP TIME: 45 minutes · COOK TIME: 15 minutes · YIELD: 18 cookies

Destined to pass over Earth once every century, Sozin's Comet endowed Firebenders with the strength and power of a hundred suns. There's no better way to celebrate this celestial body's return than with these marshmallow macarons that look like fiery comets! Okay, maybe taking down the Fire Lord and finally ending the Hundred-Year War is a slightly better way to celebrate . . . but these comet confections come close!

1 cup finely ground almond flour

1 cup powdered sugar

1 tablespoon ground cinnamon

1 teaspoon ground ginger

¼ teaspoon ground cayenne

¼ teaspoon kosher salt

3 large egg whites, at room temperature

¾ cup granulated sugar

½ teaspoon vanilla extract

6 drops orange gel food coloring

2 drops red gel food coloring, for swirling

2 drops yellow gel food coloring, for swirling

1 cup marshmallow creme

SPECIAL EQUIPMENT

Stand mixer or handheld mixer

Piping bags with round tips

Wire rack

Kitchen torch

On 2 pieces of parchment paper, using a pencil, draw 2-inch circles spaced 2 inches apart. Flip the papers over onto 2 baking sheets, placing the pencil side down.

In a medium bowl, sift the almond flour, powdered sugar, cinnamon, ginger, cayenne, and salt. Sift again. Set aside.

In the bowl of a stand mixer fitted with a whisk attachment (or in a large bowl with a handheld mixer) on medium-high speed, whip the egg whites for 2 to 3 minutes, until foamy. Slowly sprinkle in the granulated sugar and whip until just combined. Turn the speed up to high and whip for 4 to 5 minutes, until stiff peaks form. Add the vanilla and orange gel food coloring and whip until just combined. Slowly fold the dry ingredients into the egg white mixture by thirds, until the batter falls in ribbons.

Transfer the batter to a piping bag with a round tip. Pipe the macarons onto the parchment paper in uniform 2-inch circles using the drawn template.

Dip a toothpick into the red and yellow gel food coloring, then swirl into the macaron batter to create flame swirls.

Tap the baking sheet firmly on a flat surface to release air bubbles. Let the macarons sit at room temperature for 40 minutes, until dry to the touch.

Preheat the oven to 300°F.

Bake for 12 to 15 minutes, until dry. Transfer to a wire rack to cool completely.

Transfer the marshmallow creme to a piping bag with a round tip. Pipe onto the flat side of one macaron shell. Use a kitchen torch to give a slight char to the marshmallow. Top it with a second macaron shell to sandwich. Repeat with the remaining macaron shells and creme.

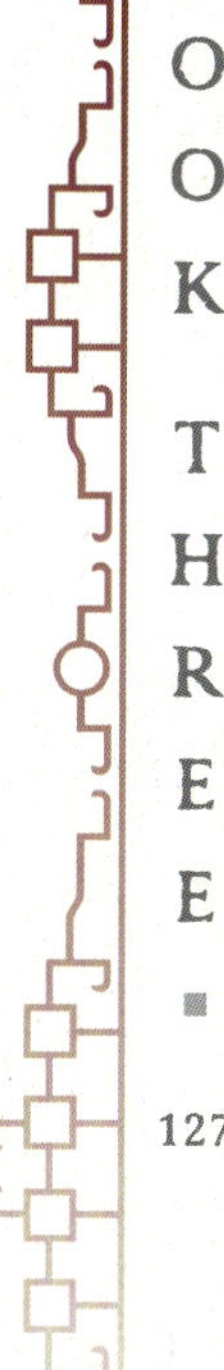

WATERMELON CAKE

V · PREP TIME: 1 hour 40 minutes, plus overnight chilling
COOK TIME: 15 minutes · YIELD: 12 servings

Who wants a nice, cool glass of watermelon juice? Even better, who wants a nice, big slice of watermelon cake? This pink cake studded with chocolate watermelon "seeds" is surprising in looks and taste. If you wanna cut yourself a piece and lounge around like a snail-sloth all day, go ahead. We won't tell!

CAKE

- 4 large eggs, separated, at room temperature
- ⅔ cup sugar, divided
- 3 tablespoons whole milk
- 2 tablespoons vegetable oil
- 1 teaspoon vanilla extract
- ½ cup cake flour
- ½ teaspoon baking powder
- ¼ teaspoon kosher salt
- ½ teaspoon cream of tartar
- 4 drops green gel food coloring, divided

SPECIAL EQUIPMENT

Kitchen paintbrush

Preheat the oven to 325°F. Line an 18-by-13-inch pan with parchment paper and coat with nonstick spray.

TO MAKE THE CAKE:

Use a clean kitchen paintbrush to add streaks of half of the green gel food coloring to the parchment paper. Set aside.

In a large bowl, whisk together the egg yolks, ⅓ cup of the sugar, milk, oil, vanilla, and remaining green gel food coloring. Add the cake flour, baking powder, and salt and whisk until just combined.

In the bowl of a stand mixer fitted with the whisk attachment (or in a large bowl with a handheld mixer) on medium-high speed, whip the egg whites and cream of tartar until fluffy. Slowly add the remaining ⅓ cup of sugar while continuing to beat the egg whites until stiff peaks form. Gently fold the whipped egg whites into the egg yolk mixture, one-third at a time, mixing until just combined. Pour the batter into the prepared baking pan.

Bake for 15 minutes, until a toothpick inserted into the center of the cake comes out clean. Let cool completely.

Flip the cake onto a clean surface. Peel off the parchment paper. Using the ring of a 9-inch springform pan as a template, along the top edge of the cake, closely cut out two 9-inch circles of cake. Set one aside and place the other into the 9-inch springform pan. Along the bottom edge of the remaining cake, cut two long strips 1½ inches tall. On top of the cake round, place one around the inside edge of the springform pan, cutting the other strip as needed to fit so the edges meet. Set aside.

FILLING

2 egg yolks

½ cup sugar

¼ teaspoon kosher salt

2 tablespoons cornstarch

1½ cups whole milk

1½ tablespoons cold water

1½ teaspoons gelatin powder

2 tablespoons strawberry jam

2 drops pink gel food coloring

1 cup heavy whipping cream

3 tablespoons mini chocolate chips

SPECIAL EQUIPMENT

18-by-13-inch pan

Stand mixer or handheld mixer

9-inch springform pan

Fine-mesh strainer

Offset spatula

TO MAKE THE FILLING:

In a large bowl, whisk together the egg yolks, sugar, and salt. Stir in the cornstarch. Set aside.

In a medium saucepan over medium-low heat, bring the milk to a simmer. Add one-third of the hot milk to the egg mixture, stirring constantly to temper. Slowly add all of the egg mixture back to the saucepan with the milk, whisking constantly until thickened. Remove from the heat and pour through a fine-mesh strainer set over a bowl. Set aside.

Pour the cold water into a separate, small bowl and sprinkle the gelatin over it. Set aside for 5 minutes, to bloom. Stir in the strawberry jam and pink gel food coloring. Set aside.

In the bowl of a stand mixer fitted with the whisk attachment (or in a large bowl with a handheld mixer) on medium speed, whip the heavy cream for 3 to 5 minutes, until light and fluffy. Fold in the gelatin mixture.

Fold the whipped cream–gelatin mixture into the custard until just combined. Fold in the mini chocolate chips. Pour the filling into the springform pan, on top of the cake, just up to the same height as the cake lining the edge of the pan. Spread evenly with an offset spatula.

Top with the second 9-inch cake round, painted side up. Cover with plastic wrap and refrigerate overnight.

Remove the plastic wrap and release the springform.

BLUBBERING BLOB MONSTER SAND SCONES

V · PREP TIME: 30 minutes · COOK TIME: 20 minutes · YIELD: 9 scones

Sokka's expertise isn't exactly in the arts, a fact he demonstrated when he tried to make a sand sculpture of Suki on the beach of Ember Island. What should have been a tribute to the Kyoshi Warrior ended up looking like a "blubbering blob monster" instead. Lucky for Sokka, Suki thought it was sweet. Hopefully, she'd think the same of these scones made in this not-so-flattering image!

SCONES

2½ cups all-purpose flour, plus more for dusting

½ cup granulated sugar

1 tablespoon matcha powder

1 tablespoon baking powder

½ teaspoon ground cinnamon

¼ teaspoon kosher salt

6 tablespoons cold unsalted butter, cubed

½ cup buttermilk

1 large egg, lightly beaten

1 teaspoon vanilla extract

GLAZE

¾ cup powdered sugar

1 tablespoon unsweetened Dutch-processed cocoa powder

1 teaspoon ground cinnamon

2 tablespoons whole milk

1 tablespoon unsalted butter, melted

DECORATIONS

9 red star sprinkles

18 sliced almonds

2 tablespoons chopped walnuts

SPECIAL EQUIPMENT

Pastry cutter

Wire rack

Preheat the oven to 400°F. Line a baking sheet with parchment paper.

TO MAKE THE SCONES:

In a large bowl, whisk together the flour, granulated sugar, matcha, baking powder, cinnamon, and salt. Use a pastry cutter to cut in the butter until crumbly. Add the buttermilk, egg, and vanilla and mix until the dough comes together.

Divide the dough into 9 equal pieces. Roll each into a ball. Transfer to the prepared baking sheet.

Bake for 18 to 20 minutes, until lightly browned. Let cool on a wire rack.

TO MAKE THE GLAZE:

In a medium bowl, whisk together the powdered sugar, cocoa powder, cinnamon, milk, and butter.

TO DECORATE:

Use the glaze to glue a star sprinkle on each scone for the nose, sliced almonds for the eyes, and chopped walnuts to create the blob monster's mouth.

Lightly drizzle the remaining glaze to create the blubbering blob monster's hair. Let the glaze set.

LION TURTLE CREAM PUFFS

V · PREP TIME: 4 hours 30 minutes · COOK TIME: 1 hour · YIELD: 12 cream puffs

While preparing for his final confrontation with Fire Lord Ozai, a conflicted Aang was drawn to a mysterious island that turned out to be the back of the wise (and sizable) lion turtle. These lion turtle pastry puffs may not contain profound words of advice or ancient knowledge that will help you win a century-long war without compromising your values . . . but the luscious cream filling inside of them is certainly worth reflecting on as you contemplate how far you've come on this epic baking journey!

CRAQUELIN

4 tablespoons unsalted butter

¼ cup sugar

⅓ cup all-purpose flour

2 teaspoons matcha powder

CHOUX PASTRY

1 cup water

½ cup (1 stick) unsalted butter

¼ teaspoon kosher salt

1 cup all-purpose flour

4 large eggs

TO MAKE THE CRAQUELIN:

In the bowl of a stand mixer fitted with the paddle attachment (or in a large bowl with a handheld mixer) on medium speed, cream the butter and sugar until fluffy. Add the flour and matcha powder and beat until just combined.

Bring the mixture together into a ball, then roll out between 2 pieces of parchment paper. Transfer (sandwiched between the parchment paper) to a baking sheet and refrigerate for 1 hour.

TO MAKE THE CHOUX PASTRY:

In a large saucepan over high heat, bring the water, butter, and salt to a boil. Decrease the heat to low, then add the flour and stir rapidly until the mixture comes together and pulls away from the sides of the saucepan.

Transfer to the bowl of a stand mixer fitted with the whisk attachment (or a large bowl with a handheld mixer) and let cool for 15 minutes.

With the mixer on low speed, add the eggs one at a time, beating until smooth. Transfer the pastry to a piping bag with a large round tip.

Preheat the oven to 375°F. Line 2 baking sheets with parchment paper.

On the baking sheets pipe a 2-inch-wide choux puff. Around the base of the puff, pipe 4 small rounds to create 4 legs, then a larger round for a head. Repeat with the remaining choux, creating 12 in total.

Remove the craquelin dough from the refrigerator and use a biscuit cutter to cut out 2-inch circles. Place a craquelin circle directly onto each choux, pressing down slightly.

Bake for 30 minutes, until golden brown. Turn off the oven, open the oven door slightly, and let sit for an additional 30 minutes.

Use a toothpick to poke a small hole into the bottom of each choux pastry to release the steam. Let cool on a wire rack.

PASTRY CREAM

2½ cups whole milk

¾ cup sugar

¼ teaspoon kosher salt

4 large egg yolks

¼ cup cornstarch

4 tablespoons unsalted butter

1 tablespoon matcha powder

1 teaspoon vanilla extract

SPECIAL EQUIPMENT

Stand mixer or handheld mixer

Piping bag with large and small round tips

2-inch biscuit cutter

Wire rack

Fine-mesh strainer

TO MAKE THE PASTRY CREAM:

In a medium saucepan over medium-low heat, bring the milk, sugar, and salt to a simmer.

In a medium bowl, whisk together the egg yolks and cornstarch. Add a ladle of the hot milk mixture to the egg yolks to temper. Place a fine-mesh strainer over the simmering milk and pour the egg yolk mixture through, back into the milk.

Bring the milk mixture to a boil, whisking constantly, until thickened. Remove from the heat. Pour through a fine-mesh strainer set over a separate large bowl. Add the butter, matcha, and vanilla and stir until combined. Place a piece of plastic wrap directly onto the surface of the pastry cream (to prevent a skin from forming). Place into the refrigerator until cool.

Remove the pastry cream from the refrigerator and transfer it to a piping bag fitted with a small round tip. Use a paring knife to cut a small hole in the bottom of each choux puff. Pipe in the pastry cream. Serve immediately.

MELON LORD HAND PIES

V · PREP TIME: 1 hour 30 minutes · COOK TIME: 25 minutes · YIELD: 8 hand pies

As Team Avatar trained for their final battle against the Fire Nation, Sokka built the Melon Lord—a practice dummy with a carved watermelon for a head. Aang may have hesitated when it came to striking down this fruit-headed foe, but you won't be able to resist decimating these pumpkin hand pies decorated with the Melon Lord's face. Consider it the tastiest training exercise ever!

DOUGH

3 cups all-purpose flour, plus more for dusting

1 tablespoon granulated sugar

½ teaspoon ground cinnamon

¼ teaspoon ground nutmeg

½ teaspoon kosher salt

1 cup (2 sticks) cold unsalted butter, cubed

8 to 10 tablespoons ice water

FILLING

½ cup pumpkin puree

4 ounces cream cheese, softened

⅓ cup packed light brown sugar

½ teaspoon ground cinnamon

¼ teaspoon ground cloves

¼ teaspoon ground ginger

¼ teaspoon ground nutmeg

¼ teaspoon kosher salt

EGG WASH

1 large egg

1 tablespoon water

TOPPING

3 tablespoons granulated sugar

1 teaspoon ground cinnamon

SPECIAL EQUIPMENT

Pastry cutter

Pastry brush

Wire rack

4-inch pumpkin-shaped cookie cutter (optional)

TO MAKE THE DOUGH:

In a large bowl, whisk together the flour, granulated sugar, cinnamon, nutmeg, and salt. Using a pastry cutter, cut the cold butter into the flour mixture until crumbly. Add the ice water, 1 tablespoon at a time, until the dough just comes together.

Divide the dough in half and pat into disks. Wrap each disk in plastic wrap and refrigerate for 30 minutes.

TO MAKE THE FILLING:

In a large bowl, add the pumpkin puree, cream cheese, brown sugar, cinnamon, cloves, ginger, nutmeg, and salt and stir until combined. Set aside.

Preheat the oven to 375°F. Line 2 baking sheets with parchment paper.

Unwrap one of the pie-dough disks. Lightly flour a work surface. Roll the dough into a rectangle about 1/16 inch thick. Cut out eight 4-inch pumpkin shapes using a cookie cutter or by hand with a sharp knife. Place 2 tablespoons of pie filling in the center of each pumpkin-shaped cutout.

Roll out the second dough disk into a rectangle about 1/16 inch thick. Cut out eight 4-inch pumpkin shapes, cutting the Melon Lord's eyes and mouth out of each one. Place these on top of the filling, pressing the edges of the top and bottom dough layers to seal.

TO MAKE THE EGG WASH:

In a small bowl, whisk together the egg and water. Brush over the hand pies.

TO MAKE THE TOPPING:

In a small bowl, whisk together the granulated sugar and cinnamon. Sprinkle over the egg wash.

Bake for 20 to 25 minutes, until golden brown. Let cool slightly on a wire rack.

CORONATION CHERRY PIE

V · PREP TIME: 40 minutes · COOK TIME: 55 minutes · YIELD: 8 servings

When Ozai crowned himself the Phoenix King, he passed the title of Fire Lord to his daughter, Princess Azula. Paranoid that she would be betrayed, Azula banished those closest to her—including a servant who accidentally left a pit in Azula's bowl of cherries. Perhaps if the poor girl had served this cherry pie instead, she would have been spared Azula's wrath . . . at least for a few more hours . . .

CRUST

2½ cups all-purpose flour, plus more for dusting

2 teaspoons granulated sugar

½ teaspoon kosher salt

1 cup (2 sticks) cold unsalted butter, cubed

8 to 10 tablespoons ice water

FILLING

3 cups frozen pitted cherries, defrosted

½ cup granulated sugar

¼ cup packed light brown sugar

¼ cup cornstarch

¼ teaspoon kosher salt

1 teaspoon lemon zest

¼ teaspoon almond extract

EGG WASH

1 large egg

1 tablespoon water

SPECIAL EQUIPMENT

Pastry cutter

9-inch pie plate

Pastry brush

Wire rack

TO MAKE THE CRUST:

In a large bowl, whisk together the flour, granulated sugar, and salt. Using a pastry cutter, cut the cold butter into the flour mixture until crumbly. Add the ice water, 1 tablespoon at a time, until the dough just comes together.

Divide the dough in half and pat into disks. Wrap each disk in plastic wrap and refrigerate for 30 minutes.

TO MAKE THE FILLING:

In a large bowl, add the cherries, granulated sugar, brown sugar, cornstarch, salt, lemon zest, and almond extract and stir until combined. Set aside.

Preheat the oven to 400°F. Coat a 9-inch pie plate with nonstick spray.

Unwrap one of the pie-dough disks. On a lightly floured surface, roll out the dough into a 13-inch circle. Transfer to the prepared pie plate, pressing the dough into the bottom and up the sides of the plate. Pour in the filling.

Roll out the second dough disk in the same way. Cut out the Fire Nation symbol from the center of the dough circle. Place the Fire Nation cutout on top of the cherry filling.

TO MAKE THE EGG WASH:

In a small bowl, whisk together the egg and water. Brush on the Fire Nation cutout.

Place the pie on a baking sheet. Lightly tent with foil. Bake for 30 minutes. Remove the foil and bake for an additional 20 minutes. Let cool completely.

CONVERSIONS

CUPS	TABLESPOONS	TEASPOONS	FLUID OUNCES
¹⁄₁₆ cup	1 tablespoon	3 teaspooons	½ fluid ounces
⅛ cup	2 tablespoons	6 teaspooons	1 fluid ounce
¼ cup	4 tablespoons	12 teaspooons	2 fluid ounces
⅓ cup	5½ tablespoons	16 teaspooons	2⅔ fluid ounces
½ cup	8 tablespoons	24 teaspooons	4 fluid ounces
⅔ cup	10⅔ tablespoons	32 teaspooons	5⅓ fluid ounces
¾ cup	12 tablespoons	36 teaspooons	6 fluid ounces
1 cup	16 tablespoons	48 teaspooons	8 fluid ounces

GALLONS	QUARTS	PINTS	CUPS	FLUID OUNCES
¹⁄₁₆ gallon	¼ quart	½ pint	1 cup	8 fluid ounces
⅛ gallon	½ quart	1 pint	2 cups	16 fluid ounces
¼ gallon	1 quart	2 pints	4 cups	32 fluid ounces
½ gallon	2 quarts	4 pints	8 cups	64 fluid ounces
1 gallon	4 quarts	8 pints	16 cups	128 fluid ounces

IMPERIAL	METRIC
1 inch	2.5 centimeters
2 inches	5 centimeters
4 inches	10 centimeters
6 inches	15 centimeters
8 inches	20 centimeters
10 inches	25 centimeters

GRAMS	OUNCES
14 grams	½ ounce
28 grams	1 ounce
57 grams	2 ounces
85 grams	3 ounces
113 grams	4 ounces
142 grams	5 ounces
170 grams	6 ounces
283 grams	10 ounces
397 grams	14 ounces
454 grams	16 ounces
907 grams	32 ounces

FAHRENHEIT	CELSUIS
200°F	93°C
225°F	107°C
250°F	121°C
275°F	135°C
300°F	149°C
325°F	163°C
350°F	177°C
375°F	191°C
400°F	204°C
425°F	218°C
450°F	232°C

ABOUT THE AUTHORS

JENN FUJIKAWA is a lifestyle and pop-culture author, content creator, and host. She has created content for Lucasfilm, Marvel, Disney, and more. Jenn is the author of multiple fandom-based cookbooks, including *Star Wars: The Life Day Cookbook*, *Gremlins: The Official Cookbook*, *Ghostbusters: The Official Cookbook*, *Parks and Recreation: The Official Cookbook*, *The Princess Bride: The Official Cookbook*, and many more. For more of her recipes, check out her Instagram @justjennrecipes.

MARC SUMERAK has spent over two decades crafting story content for some of the most celebrated brands in entertainment, including Marvel, Star Wars, and more. He has coauthored a variety of cookbooks, including *Star Wars: Galaxy's Edge—The Official Black Spire Outpost Cookbook*, *Star Wars: The Life Day Cookbook*, *Avengers Campus: The Official Cookbook*, and *The Office: The Official Party Planning Guide to Planning Parties*. His work has also appeared in countless books, comics, and video games. He resides in Cleveland, Ohio.

ACKNOWLEDGMENTS

Thank you to my family, who encouraged me to harness my Airbender prowess: Alice Kawakami; Kyle, Tyler, and Mason Fujikawa; and Mark Kawakami. To all the Avatars who helped me along the way: Mel Caylo, Cheryl deCarvalho, Chrissy Dinh, Chrys Hasegawa, Kyle Kao and Kim Trinidad, Sarah Kuhn, and Robb Pearlman. Thank you to the team at Nickelodeon, especially Raina Moore. Thanks also to Elena Craig. To Marc Sumerak, my partner on this airbending journey. To the Air Acolyte who kept me on track: Alexis Sattler. Final words of wisdom for my kids: Watch out for loose cabbages.

Jenn Fujikawa

Thanks to Jenn Fujikawa for being the Katara to my Sokka on all of our culinary adventures together. Thanks to Alexis Sattler for providing guidance and wisdom on par with Uncle Iroh. Thanks to Charlie and Lincoln for never letting me lose sight of why I'm on this crazy journey in the first place. And thanks to all the fascinating strangers out there. Sharing this book with you is one of life's true delights.

Marc Sumerak

INDEX

PO Box 3088
San Rafael, CA 94912
www.insighteditions.com

Find us on Facebook: www.facebook.com/InsightEditions

Follow us on Instagram: @insighteditions

ISBN: 979-8-88663-824-0

Publisher: Raoul Goff
SVP, Group Publisher: Vanessa Lopez
VP, Creative: Chrissy Kwasnik
VP, Manufacturing: Alix Nicholaeff
Publishing Director: Mike Degler
Editorial Director: Thom O'Hearn
Art Director: Stuart Smith
Senior Designer: Brooke McCullum
Editor: Alexis Sattler
Associate Editor: Sami Alvarado
Editorial Assistant: Gabrielle Cruz
Managing Editor: Shannon Ballesteros
Production Manager: Deena Hashem
Strategic Production Planner: Lina s Palma-Temena

Photography: Ted Thomas
Food and Prop Styling: Elena P. Craig
Food Styling Assistant: Haley Garrett
Food Styling Assistant: Patricia Parrish
Food Styling Assistant: August Craig

NICKELODEON

Designer: Micol Hiatt
Senior Editorial Director: Raina Moore

SPECIAL THANKS

Executive Editor: Joan Hilty, Avatar Studios

Insight Editions, in association with Roots of Peace, will plant two trees for each tree used in the manufacturing of this book. Roots of Peace is an internationally renowned humanitarian organization dedicated to eradicating land mines worldwide and converting war-torn lands into productive farms and wildlife habitats. Roots of Peace will plant two million fruit and nut trees in Afghanistan and provide farmers there with the skills and support necessary for sustainable land use.

Manufactured in China by Insight Editions

10 9 8 7 6 5 4 3 2 1